"Resituating and extending M
Communism into vibrant new
a clear passion for a city and
radical political potentials that ᴖ ᴖ ᴖ ᴖ ᴖᴖᴖ ᴖᴖ ᴖᴖ ᴖᴖ ᴖᴖ only in
its past but, perhaps even more importantly, in its present
and proximate future."

Matt Colquhoun, author of *Egress: On Mourning,*
Melancholy and Mark Fisher

"Through the toxic runoff of snowed-in flyover country and
psychedelic outsiderism, Joe Molloy untangles the creative
minds that go fast and furiously into new musical territories
while honoring the decades of untouchable classics that
came before. *Acid Detroit* is a music lover's insider look into
the sublime joy of seeing time catch up to itself... we also
never thought we'd see a mosh pit at a Gories show!"

Will Lorenz, The Stools

"This gave me so much knowledge of the history of music
in Detroit, and made me so proud to be a part of our city's
history and culture."

Bruiser Wolf

"Joe Molloy's in-depth and emotionally charged writing,
specifically about John Brannon's career, really pulls in
and enraptures the reader. You can tell by the attention to
detail how much research and heart has been put into this
book on Detroit music."

Joey Hanania, Toeheads

ACID DETROIT

ACID DETROIT

A PSYCHEDELIC STORY OF MOTOR CITY MUSIC

Joe Molloy

Published by Repeater Books

An imprint of Watkins Media Ltd

Unit 11 Shepperton House

89-93 Shepperton Road

London

N1 3DF

United Kingdom

www.repeaterbooks.com

A Repeater Books paperback original 2023

1

Distributed in the United States by Random House, Inc., New York.

Copyright © Joe Molloy 2023

Joe Molloy asserts the moral right to be identified as the author of this work.

ISBN: 9781914420511

Ebook ISBN: 9781914420528

Printed and bound in the United Kingdom by TJ Books Limited

CONTENTS

0. PRELUDE

What is Acid Detroit?

There are many books on Detroit music history, but none are quite like the one you are holding now. While others have dug deep into specific moments in the city's history, this is the first book to survey the entire territory, setting out to cover the terrain of six decades worth of musical history. *Acid Detroit* is an attempt to trace a through line from the early days of Motown to the birth of punk and techno, up through the creative efflorescence of the present day. In the process of tracing the city's rich musical legacy, we'll also point to an underlying philosophical — often psychedelic — ethos that unifies the musicians of Detroit.

No history can contain everything, and — crucially — the storyteller decides what might be included and excluded. In *Acid Detroit*, for example, you'll find that some of the most well-known musicians from Detroit — Bob Seger, Eminem and Kid Rock — are either paid a passing glance or not mentioned at all. Meanwhile, lesser-discussed artists like the Supremes, Laughing Hyenas and the Gories get plenty of space on the page.

It is my hope that this book persuades people to listen to some of the most life-affirming music in the world. That's the goal of *Acid Detroit*, plain and simple. Working as a record store clerk and amateur radio DJ in college, I've come to realize that nothing moves me quite like sharing music with people. So, if this book gets one person to fall in love with the Supremes' *Where Did Our Love Go*, Cybotron's *Clear* or Danny Brown's *Atrocity Exhibition*, then I'll consider *Acid Detroit* a success. Setting my sights higher, my hope is that this book will inspire a radically new popular perception of Detroit. Not as a city of crushed dreams, but as a resilient bastion of consistent, cutting-edge American culture. Detroit is a city full of people brimming with brilliance and innovation.

Acid Detroit names the music of Detroit, its motoric pulse and soulful energy, as what bleeds out of and dissolves the drudgery of the city's once-prosperous industries. In doing so, *Acid Detroit* also points to the notion that the spirit of the counterculture — politically, sonically, aesthetically — never left Detroit. Thus, we can use the city's music history as a roadmap for teasing out new futures and inspiring alternative ways of living. But before the music starts, let's quickly lay the philosophical groundwork for our tale and look at the "Acid" in *Acid Detroit*.

The Specter of a World Which Could Be Free

In late 2016, before his tragic passing by suicide, the British cultural theorist Mark Fisher was fleshing out the ideas for his next book — tentatively titled *Acid Communism* — with a group of students at Goldsmiths University in London on a module he convened called "Post-Capitalist Desire." This new notion of "acid communism" found Fisher assessing lost revolutionary potentials of the 1960s and 1970s. This was perceived as a shocking move for those within Fisher's circle, considering he had previously written disparagingly of the counterculture and its hedonistic refusal to engage with real social problems. Yet, if acid communism — or "psychedelic socialism", as his friend and collaborator Jeremy Gilbert first called it — points to anything, it is a project dedicated to resituating, recontextualizing and renegotiating the past. In actuality, the concept is a natural extension of Fisher's ideas around hauntology — the mourning of lost futures — and capitalist realism — the pervasive sense that we can no longer envision alternatives to capitalism. If his 2009 surprise bestseller *Capitalist Realism: Is There No Alternative?* was a diagnosis of the disease and 2014's collection of earlier essays, *Ghosts of My Life*, was a process of identifying its symptoms, then *Acid Communism* would perhaps be the first attempt at a cure.

All that survived of Fisher's would-be book on psychedelic socialism is an uncompleted introduction that has steadily garnered something of a dedicated cult readership. The cryptic and unfinished nature of the work has led many to ponder on what lines of flight Fisher's psychedelic strategy would have set course for. The question lingers, then: what is this neologism really pointing to? We don't need to speculate too much. Fisher himself clearly defined acid communism in what he had written:

> Acid communism is a provocation and a promise. It is a joke of sorts, but one with a very serious purpose. It points to something that, at one point, seemed inevitable, but which now appears impossible: *the convergence of class consciousness, socialist-feminist consciousness-raising and psychedelic consciousness, the fusion of new social movements with a communist project, an unprecedented aestheticization of everyday life.*

Acid communism seeks to excavate and reclaim — often purposely erased — elements of the counterculture in order to see what they might offer us in our troubled times of contemporary capitalist realism. If hauntology focused on modernism's ineradicable trace, then acid communism looked to the counterculture as a counter-narrative. The counterculture represented a surge of libidinal, cathartic and transformational consciousness-expanding before the neoliberal 1970s swooped in to deflate it. With the thwarted development of the countercultural subject, the neoliberal project reasserted the dominance of capital, markets and middle-class family values, all the while co-opting and channeling those hedonistic and communal impulses into a corporatized California ideology.

If Fisher identified the specters haunting our world, those specters in turn inevitably haunt Fisher's work, and first among them he was — albeit subconsciously — haunted by Detroit. It is perhaps Detroit that best encapsulates the rise and fall of the hopes of modernity. In Detroit we see the social and psychic costs of having been at the core of the Fordist post-war project, as well as the ruinous edge of neoliberal globalization. Simultaneously, it is here we see the ways in which wider continuities of resilience, community and aesthetics have stayed true to a certain form of countercultural desire, sowing among the ruins the seeds of emergent post-capitalist futures. Fisher was of course aware of the radical potentials lurking behind Detroit's obscured music history and all his ground-breaking formulations will be useful in guiding us — either implicitly or explicitly — on our journey through the city's musical legacy. Hauntology — the mourning of lost futures — can best be exemplified by the broken promise of a utopian city brought on by Fordism, and his conception of "the eerie" will serve us in sifting through that city's ruins. Ultimately, with his turn toward post-capitalist desires and acid communism, he explicitly returns to Detroit itself to reflect on the radical potential the city always possessed — looking at the sonic innovations of the Temptations and Norman Whitfield — in order to point us toward its future.

In his book *The Weird and The Eerie,* Fisher wrote of the eerie as being marked by the sensation that "there's something present where there should be nothing, or there's nothing present where there should be something."

4

Detroit is a fundamentally eerie zone, its deindustrialized automotive factories and decaying monumental civic architecture an exemplary site of the perverse libidinal energy expressed by the term "ruin porn." In one of Fisher's favorite films, Andrei Tarkovsky's 1979 *Stalker*, a trio of seekers make a journey through an elusive, derelict site called the Zone. Inside the Zone, the laws of physics no longer apply and reality as we know it begins to break down. Before our very eyes, what at first appeared to be an entrapment becomes a safe passageway. The geography of an open field of junk can turn in on itself, potentially spawning something sublime, monstrous or banal. At the core of the Zone lies a room in which a person's deepest, innermost desires will be granted. This is an example of Fisher's concept of "the Weird," which is marked by an exorbitant, brimming presence "of that which does not belong." The city of Detroit offers up a similar proposition. Long a symbol of capitalistic neglect, Detroit has been treated as a sort of taboo zone within America, and certainly within the state of Michigan. However, once inside the city, one sees that it is unlike any other place in the world, and those who have experienced it know that within the city — like the Zone in *Stalker* — lies something sublime and transcendental.

Considering the phantom thread of Detroit that runs throughout his work, it is natural that Fisher himself accompanies us in spectral form, both as passenger and guide, as we explore the multi-layered psychedelic confluence of interleaved and disorienting temporal and spatial folds that compose *Acid Detroit*. In Detroit, the ruins, remains and specters evoke — even invoke — the Fordist pop-soul machine Motown, the mind-melting death rock of the late Sixties and Seventies, the ghostly machine-funk of techno, the turbocharged garage-punk bands of post-Fordism, and bleed across the boundary into the city's current efflorescence of new musical forms. What emerges is an unapologetically modernist trajectory where the city's musicians continually quest after the new while simultaneously trying to absorb the loss of a monumental past. At each stop along our journey through Detroit space-time, we'll attempt to tease out these radical possibilities that still lurk beneath the scorched earth of the past sixty years.

1. MASS PRODUCING THE PLEASURES: FORDISM AND MOTOWN

As I rode back to Detroit, a vision of Henry Ford's industrial empire kept passing before my eyes. In my ears, I heard the wonderful symphony which came from his factories where metals were shaped into tools for men's service. It was a new music, waiting for the composer with genius enough to give it communicable form.

Diego Rivera, *My Art My Life*

Motor City is inhabited with ghosts of both the city's past and future. If there can be said to be one specter that haunts the city's psyche most relentlessly, it is that of Henry Ford. It's with Ford, therefore, that this ghost story begins. The story of Ford is one that harkens back to a deep mythological past when the notion of the American dream was the prevailing ideology of the day.

Ford was born in Springwells Township, Michigan, in 1863. From the beginning, he was a tinkerer and took it upon himself to learn what he did not already know. In 1908, after founding the Ford Motor Company in Detroit, he would create the world's first affordable, easily maintainable and mass-produced automobile — the Model T. An extremely important development, contributing to the success of both the Ford Motor Company and of the Model T, was Ford's introduction of the assembly line at his Highland Park plant in 1913, and later to the other plants in Detroit. Ford had envisioned that the building of cars would function most efficiently along stationed points of a conveyor belt. Moving from team to team, the building process could be simplified, streamlined and its speed greatly increased, with workers specializing in one specific aspect of the automobile's construction. This simple but ingenious idea led to the Ford Motor Company becoming the largest automobile manufacturer in America, with the Model T accounting for over half the cars driven in the USA by 1918. It then spread across nearly all manufacturing industries, with it eventually being dubbed "Fordism," after its creator. As a result, Detroit became the automobile hub of the world and the seat of the American industrial empire — and Motor City was born.

Another aspect of Fordism was Henry Ford's labor philosophy — his workers worked a five-day week, giving them the ability to luxuriate on the weekends and spend time with their families, and were paid a $5 wage (approximately $30 by today's numbers), which broke with the tradition of paying factory laborers slave wages. These incentives attracted the best and brightest engineers from across America, equipping Ford and the other Detroit companies now following suit with one of the most efficient workforces in the country.

It was the Italian Marxist Antonio Gramsci who first coined the term "Fordism" to describe this set of factors that made up Ford's new form of assembly-line capitalism. As Richard Seymour notes in an excellent blog post on Fordism and Motown, Gramsci "perceived Fordism as a relatively progressive tendency away from individualism and competition, toward planning and cooperation." Indeed, Fordism greatly changed the material conditions of factory workers. For the first time, laborers were afforded the basic luxuries of life. However, Ford's philosophy wasn't entirely altruistic. In fact, his motives for raising pay and shortening the working week were dubious at best. For the same reason he was willing to employ African

Americans, Ford implemented the programs as a means of keeping his workers quelled and under his control. This goes hand in hand with Ford being staunchly anti-union. The fact that Ford forbid and did what he could to suppress union strength is perhaps the most clear-cut way of showing that Ford was not really a champion of worker power and solidarity. Indeed, Ford claimed he would *never* allow his workers to unionize and went to great lengths in attempting to make this the case.

In 1932, the Mexican artist Diego Rivera arrived in Detroit with his wife, the blossoming painter Frida Kahlo, on assignment. He was commissioned by Edsel Ford — Henry's son and a Ford executive — to grace the walls of the Detroit Institute of Arts' central, open-air courtyard with a mural honoring the city. As the industrial leader of the country, the new museum, opened five years prior in 1927, was to be a reflection of Detroit's cultural dominance too. However, the Great Depression was in full swing, and the Motor City that Kahlo and Rivera visited was less utopian than Ford had promised.

The first factory Rivera visited for inspiration was the iconic River Rouge Plant. Certainly, the tour was a tense one. Just days before Rivera's arrival in Detroit, the Ford Hunger March, or Massacre, had occurred. Supported by the Unemployed Councils and the Communist Party, protestors demanding jobs, stability and fair pay had begun marching to the plant when they were attacked by Ford's security forces. In the shootout, four workers were killed and over sixty were injured. Months later, a fifth worker died from their injuries. The massacre was just one of many instances across Detroit history where the unseen, raw power of capital would reveal itself to devastating effect. Of course, the protest was justified. At the time of Rivera's visit, welfare was only fifteen cents a day, which equates to a little less than five dollars in 2022. Despite these discouraging conditions, Rivera saw a light at the end of the tunnel. In fact, he saw Fordism as providing the automation and efficiency necessary to bring about a socialist state. As Rivera himself put it:

> Marx made theory... Lenin applied it with his sense of large-scale social organization... And Henry Ford made the work of the socialist state possible.

For Rivera, the machinery needed to produce a utopian dream city was here, just in the wrong hands.

Rivera and Kahlo were both long-time members of the Mexican Communist Party and believed in championing the industrial proletariat as agents in a forthcoming revolution of inconceivable social and psychic magnitude. Rivera had joined in 1922, while a twenty-year-old Kahlo joined in 1927. A decade later, in 1937, after convincing the Mexican government, the pair would welcome banished Soviet revolutionary Leon Trotsky to their country for asylum. As a communist, Rivera saw his art as a revolutionary tool that he could use to critique the system from within. Indeed, Rivera was a wolf in sheep's clothing, doing the bidding of corporate capitalists on his own terms. He looked at Detroit through the eyes of a man thinking not about glorifying the individual capitalist, but about liberation and revolution. Rivera held the belief that public art contained the potential to shift society, raise consciousness and ultimately change society for the better. After eleven months of work, he unveiled the twenty-seven-panel work entitled *The Detroit Industry Murals.* The staggering fresco, in Rivera's signature social-realist style, depicts a swarm of diverse workers on the automobile factory floor, stationed along the Fordist assembly line. In keeping with Rivera's political allegiances, the tableaux brims with Marxist themes of proletarian solidarity and dignity. Here, Rivera depicts man and machine working together in harmony.

Despite the gloom of the Depression, Rivera saw fit to endow the mural with a theme that persists in the city to this day — rebirth. Central to the mural, placed above the spectator as they walk deeper into the museum, is the image of an infant, planted like a seedling in the womb of the Earth's soil. Above the factory mural — the defining image of the high Fordist system — are human figures laying, outstretched and dignified. Above them are hands emerging out of the land. This is a city of rebirth. Infused with the mural are visions of the Earth, the natural and green. Here, Rivera points out the interconnectedness of man, machine and nature.

To this day, Rivera's mural is etched into the walls of the courtyard, a constant reminder of the cycles of life and death the city has gone through. It serves as an important symbol of Detroit iconography, and inspires the city's residents who return to it year after year. Within the mural is simultaneously a haunting glimpse of the past and a roadmap for the future. In it, we have the first glimpse of a psychedelic socialism and revolution in consciousness — the commitment to hope — needed to upend the system. This is the nascent formation of an acid communism, the specter of a world which could be free.

If there is another figure to whom we also might attribute the increased prosperity of the workers in Detroit, it is Walter Reuther. Emerging out of this same historical milieu, Reuther was a working-class hero who organized protests, strikes and walkouts in the mid-1930s against the "Big Three" automakers — General Motors, Chrysler and Ford. As president of the United Auto Workers, Reuther was instrumental in fighting for an increasingly better quality of work and benefits. He was a progressive leader, championed civil rights and made it so that factory workers could enjoy middle-class luxuries. His consistent commitment to these values over time would lend him the opportunity decades later, in 1963, to speak at Martin Luther King Jr.'s March on Washington, where he crucially connected the struggle for equal rights with organized labor. It is this interplay of forces, rather than Ford's generosity and business acumen alone, that drives the unprecedented growth, prosperity and monumentality of Detroit up to its peak in the 1960s, and it's the collapse of that dynamic tension that leads on into the decline and spectacle of its subsequent collapse.

Gramsci, writing while imprisoned in Fascist Italy, brooding in his cell, was something of a prophet who foresaw how the Fordist system would end, predicting the deterioration, the abandonment, the decay of the machines. Firstly, he noted that the industrialist-capitalist system would still lead to massive inequality. Indeed, Gramsci observed that

> Monopoly wages correspond to monopoly profits. But the monopoly will necessarily be first limited and then destroyed by the further diffusion of the new methods both within the United States and abroad (compare the Japanese phenomenon of low-priced goods), and high wages will disappear along with enormous profits.

Recognizing this, Gramsci goes on to note that the crisis consists "precisely in the fact that the old is dying and the new cannot be born, [and] in this interregnum a great variety of morbid symptoms appear."

In Detroit, the mid-1960s were a time of consciousness-raising with revolutionary groups sprouting up. The Black Panthers wouldn't arrive in Detroit until 1968, so militants were homegrown and formed their own collectives. Examples of such groups were Detroit's League of Revolutionary Black Workers and the Dodge Revolutionary Union

Movement, or DRUM for short. In 1965, their activities are crucially documented in the collectively directed 1970 film *Finally Got the News*. The film is primarily composed of ideological lectures from members of the league, overlaid with footage that takes us to the grinding factory floor and the homes they organize at in their free time — the worlds of praxis and theory respectively. The film opens with a Soviet-style montage that traces the history of racial capitalism in the United States. By linking the slaves of the South with African American auto factory workers, the film immediately asserts the thesis that industrial capitalism is a continued form of enslavement that requires exploitable bodies. Reinforcing this opening montage is the first line of dialogue. In a room with posters of Marxist revolutionaries like Che Guevara and Mao Zedong plastered on the walls, a lecturing worker states:

> Black workers have historically been the foundation stone upon which the American industrial empire has been built and sustained. It began with slavery over four-hundred years ago when black people were captured on the West coast of Africa, shipped to the United States, what was then the colonies, and used to produce surplus value.

In *Finally Got the News*, we have one of the most valuable documents of the era's political militancy as we see organized black workers in action, leafleting and on the picket line, attempting to circumvent the corrupt bureaucracies that plague the UAW and factory. The film is a reminder that, although the 1960s are often recalled as the height of Detroit, there were still serious issues that needed to be fought and organized against and, indeed, black working-class history and struggle has been and remains uniquely central to all facets of Detroit life.

A specter is haunting Detroit — the specter of the Fordist

empire's utopian project. Its remnants are everywhere in the city. On a late-night drive through its vast, empty streets, Detroit might itself seem to be, in an uncanny collapsing of time into space, the very interregnum of which Gramsci spoke — an eerily timeless city, one *made* eerie by the continuous motions of capitalism, suspended between eras and in which many pasts, presents and futures are overlaid. Though, as we'll see, that lost utopian city is still preserved elsewhere, embedded deep within the grooves of its vinyl records.

Assembly Line Soul

At the plant cars started out as just a frame, pulled along on conveyor belts until they emerged at the end of the line — brand spanking new cars rolling off the line. I wanted the same concept for my company, only with artists and songs and records. I wanted a place where a kid off the street could walk in one door an unknown and come out another a recording artist — a star.
Berry Gordy Jr., *To Be Loved*

Detroit was always a great music town, and always will be. Though our story of Motor City music will pick up with the emergence of Motown, we ought to note that Detroit was a rich musical hub all throughout the first half of the twentieth century. In the 1920s, the city had one of the best blues scenes in America, but because there was no recording industry set up, many artists went to Chicago to record. During the second wave of the Great Migration in the 1940s, Detroit welcomed a great number of African American blues musicians from the Deep South. Perhaps the most prominent player was John Lee Hooker, who ignited the style of music with a whole new life when he recorded his electrifying tune "Boogie Chillen" at Detroit's United Sound studios. With an amplified guitar riff and beat supplied by his incessant foot-tapping, Hooker would inspire a million musicians around the country. He certainly set off a chain reaction. Bursting out of the gates in April of 1954, Detroit son Bill Haley would kickstart America's rock 'n roll craze with one of the decade's defining songs, "Rock Around the Clock."

In the realm of jazz, Detroit was responsible for producing greats like the mighty trumpeter Donald Byrd, bassist Paul Chambers and drummer Elvin Jones, who endowed the city with a sense of swing. The ruling record label of this pre-Motown period was Fortune Records, which released doo-wop tunes from Nolan Strong & the Diablos, whom Smokey Robinson would cite as his foremost vocal influence. Fortune also found success with Nathaniel Mayer, a musician who, decades later, would link up with members of the Dirtbombs, a Detroit garage rock project we'll discuss in chapter six. All of this serves to show that Detroit was always a great music city, but it wasn't until the arrival of a businessman with a formula for hit singles that the whole world began to look to the Motor City as America's music hub.

That man, Berry Gordy Jr., is responsible for delivering some of the most euphoric music of the twentieth century. Curiously, he had an inauspicious start. His father, Berry Gordy II, migrated to Detroit from Georgia hoping to evade racism and the violence of the Ku Klux Klan, as he had become a target after making too much money. Detroit was a natural relocation choice because of the booming automotive industry and the prospect of economic prosperity offered up by the plants. As a father, Gordy II instilled the hardworking mentality and core principles of capitalist ideology in his sons. This notion — that one could make a fortune by owning the means of production — was perhaps best exemplified in the mythical success story of Detroit's Henry Ford. The basic idea would take hold in his son, Berry Gordy III, who would apply the capitalist ethos to music, in the process creating the most lucrative black-owned business in America.

As a young boy, Berry Gordy Jr. enjoyed music, but his real passion was boxing. In eleventh grade, he decided to make a run at a professional career in what Joyce Carol Oates called "the cruelest sport", dropping out of high school. Gordy's dream of quick riches and fame was thwarted shortly after when he was drafted to serve in the Korean War in 1951. Though he had to move on, the fierce, uncompromising spirit of an ice-veined boxer would remain part of his ethos. Arriving on Korean soil in 1952, his foundational love for music would resurface. Taking the role of a chaplain's assistant, Gordy played the organ at religious services. Conjuring up visions of Detroit churches' stained-glass shrines, Gordy's organ playing provided gospel music for the soldiers.

Upon returning home in 1953, Gordy married Thelma Louise Coleman and ran a failing jazz record shop. When the shop went out of business, it would lead Gordy to do what any Detroiter seeking work would — get a job at the auto factory. In Gordy's case, that meant working on the line of the Lincoln-Mercury plant. But he still held onto his musical dreams as an aspiring songwriter. Composing songs quite literally to the rhythm of the plant, Gordy's music embodied Detroit's philosophy of man merging with machines. Writing songs with his sister Gwen, the sibling duo would score a minor hit in 1957 with "Reet Petite," recorded by Billy Davis; they would also write the Etta James tune "All I Could Do Was Cry." Reinvesting his money from the plant and songwriting successes into production work, Gordy fatefully discovered the Miracles, a small group led by the mesmerizing Smokey Robinson. With his increasing success and desire to cultivate artists' careers, Gordy now had his sights set on something bigger — a record label.

With Smokey's moral support and his family's financial support, Gordy created Tamla Records in 1959 and that same year purchased Motown's headquarters — a house on 2648 West Grand Boulevard that he would call Hitsville, USA. Inside Hitsville, Gordy made a studio and organized the space so that it would mirror the efficiency of the auto factories he had worked in. Now a preserved site of Detroit history, Hitsville serves as a Motown Museum. On 14 April 1960, Gordy would merge Tamla and his new Motown label into one entity: Motown Record Corporation.

The ascendance of Motown Records parallels the story of the Ford Motor Company. Like Henry Ford, the story of Motown's Berry Gordy is one of achieving the mythological American Dream. Similarly, Motown revolutionized its respective industry — making hit records — by applying the Fordist formula of the assembly line to music production. This revolutionary approach could have only been born in Detroit, where the Fordist process was embedded in the structure of daily life. We can imagine the young Berry working at the Ford factory, watching the cars move from station to station, and dreaming up a machinic process of producing perfect cultural artifacts. Putting it all together, Gordy ingeniously realized that — like the car conveyor belts in the factories — music-making could also move along an assembly line from A&R men to songwriters to recording engineers to producers to song selectors to art packagers and finally distributors. The result made Detroit simultaneously both the industrial and cultural capital of the country, and arguably the world.

Whether we're looking as far back as slaves singing field hollers throughout the 1800s or the gospel arrangements of the Fisk Jubilee Singers, or even up to the more modern stylings of 2 Live Crew and Bell Biv Devoe, group singing has always been an enduring element of African American music-making. As an expression of community and solidarity, collective singing connects African Americans with each other and reveals the power of coming together. From the outset, we see that, with groups like the Temptations and the Supremes, the desire for Motown — some of the best music to ever exist — is also the desire for collectivism. It is music culture that showcases the desire to shift away from the archetypal lone-wolf genius in favor of communities, scenes and collaborative art experiments. The British experimental musician and father of ambient Brian Eno calls it "*scenius*" — the transference of genius from one great individual to a group of unique contributors that form something bigger than oneself. As we'll see, this theme of collectivism runs through Detroit's musical history and is the bedrock for the city's consistently cohesive musical scenes.

Motown therefore had a wealth of brilliance right in its backyard. The label introduced the world to legendary Detroit locals such as Marvin Gaye, the Supremes, Smokey Robinson & the Miracles, the Temptations, "Little" Stevie Wonder and the Four Tops. Also from the Midwest, Gordy signed the Jackson 5, writing the hits that would present to the world Michael Jackson and his brothers. Coming in from Atlanta, Gordy got Gladys Knight & the Pips on the label. Aretha Franklin was also from the area at the same time, but she would sign elsewhere, taking her transcendental gospel-soul to New York City.

In the distinct "Motown Sound," we hear traces of pop, soul, gospel and rock, but the records have such a distinct hair-raising quality that they constitute their own domain. Motown's producers utilized the "wall of sound" pioneered by Phil Spector without overcomplicating things. In fact, simplicity was central to the production process, as producers strictly adhered to the "K.I.S.S." principle (Keep It Simple, Stupid). In a seemingly paradoxical vein, by using the Fordist formula, Motown cranked out machinic pop-perfection that inspired intense feelings of joy and a love for humanity.

In its early years, Motown had emerged as one of the most promising labels in the country, and 1964 marked that watershed moment when the women of Hitsville, USA, solidified Motown as *the* greatest label in the world. That year the label released four number-one singles, three of which were attributed to the Supremes: "Where Did Our Love Go," "Baby Love" and "Come See About Me." In all of these songs, the combination of Diana Ross's angelic croon and flawlessly calculated chord changes condensed into a two-minute single is euphoric.

When Dr. Cornel West spoke in Detroit at a Bernie Sanders rally in 2020, he noted that McCoy Tyner of the John Coltrane quartet had passed away. Tyner had played on John Coltrane's jazz touchstone *A Love Supreme*, a record that is said to be a message straight to God, a direct dispatch to the heavens. If *A Love Supreme* is a message to the higher power, I like to imagine the Supremes as what the angels' response would sound like: something so beautiful that everything else pales in comparison.

1964 also saw the release of Mary Wells' number-one hit single "My Guy." Then, in the heat of that year's July, Martha & the Vandellas called out around the world with their anthemic "Dancing in the Street." Later, amidst the consumerist Christmas spending rush that December, the Temptations released "My Girl," which would hit number one in the new year of 1965. With the Motown machine operating at full capacity, the Temptations would go on to be one of the label's — and the city's — biggest success stories.

In their classic period — 1964 through 1972 — the Temptations were composed of founder Otis Williams, bass singer Melvin Franklin, arranger and stylist Eddie

Kendricks, choreographer Paul Williams and the tortured, raspy-voiced David Ruffin. When the collective put their voices and extra abilities together, they transformed into something greater than the sum of their parts. Descending from the lineage of classy crooners that came before them like the Rat Pack, the group's impeccable style, grooming and swagger made them emblems of 1960s cool. With a string of hit singles to boot, they were a ubiquitous presence on the charts earning them respect as "The Emperors of Soul."

We'll return to the Temptations — a band central to Fisher's thinking about Acid Communism — in a later chapter, but first, in order to cover the scope and simultaneous diversity and depth of what was going on in Detroit in the 1960s, we'll take a quick detour through a rather different but equally central genre to the Motor City's musical history, a predominantly "white" musical form, but one which I'll argue, in Detroit's case, is in constant exchange with the city's black musical heritage, traditions and artists — garage rock.

2. THIS IS DETROIT, NOT LA:
REVOLUTIONARY PROTO PUNKERS

In one of the most famous meditations on the death of the 1960s, gonzo journalist Hunter S. Thompson wrote in *Fear and Loathing in Las Vegas* that:

> there was madness in any direction, at any hour. [...] You could strike sparks anywhere. [...] We had all the momentum; we were riding the crest of a high and beautiful wave. [...] So now, less than five years later, you can go up a steep hill in Las Vegas and look West, and with the right kind of eyes you can almost see the high-water mark — that place where the wave finally broke and rolled back.

Reflecting on the end of that righteous decade in her seminal essay, "The White Album," the countercultural literary icon Joan Didion wrote:

> Many people I know in Los Angeles believe that the Sixties ended abruptly on August 9, 1969, ended at the exact moment when word of the murders on Cielo Drive travelled like brushfire through the community, and in a sense that is true.

Indeed, the dark shadow of Charles Manson's helter-skelter chaos death ritual looms large in hippie history.

In fact, the Manson murders were so decisive that it has invited many to ask whether the unquestioning free-love psychedelia of the Sixties would have ever ended had they not occurred. This question is the entire conceit of Quentin Tarantino's love letter to the decade, his 2019 film *Once Upon a Time in Hollywood*. It is a classic case of cathartic alternate history, ending in a glorious flamethrowing crescendo where Leonardo DiCaprio and Brad Pitt prevent the Manson cult from carrying out the murder of Sharon Tate. Yet this type of fixation on Manson suggests that the decade of flower-power eccentrics exclusively took place in Los Angeles. Adding to the case for the prosecution, the aforementioned Thompson and Didion — the hometown hero of Sacramento — were both Californian writers.

Reflecting on this, according to Fisher in *Acid Communism*:

> The Sixties counterculture is now inseparable from its own simulation, and the reduction of the decade to "iconic" images, to "classic" music and to nostalgic reminiscences has neutralized the real promises that exploded then.

Fisher is right — we have in some sense not just collectively *displaced* the 1960s, but actually *mis-placed* them. We return to the right time period, but are rerouted to the wrong place, continually locating the central hub of 1960s revolutionary potential in California, or for European readers in Paris in May 1968. This is a white-centric misremembering, which places all the emphasis on the iconic-symbolic.

When we say the 1960s died in California, it raises the question of what world collapsed and for whom? Increasingly, what is mourned in the death of the Sixties is a certain lifestyle, largely the one of lethargic, hedonic lassitude: strung out on dope by the beach, turning away from collectivity in favor of solipsistic bliss, disengaging with real social problems, and an underlying sexism at the core of male hippies' insistence on unquestioning free love. In the process, we reduce the 1960s to Jefferson

Airplane posters, tie-dye tapestry and the sunset strip. The decade becomes *Once Upon A Time in Hollywood* — a diluted joyride, always shirking a confrontation with the Real. In Tarantino's film, Manson's 1969 murders are even thwarted. This presupposes California actually died in some way. Certainly, it's understandable that paranoia crept in for a time, but in reality, Los Angeles remained the site of wealth, cultural capital and privilege we still know today. Meanwhile, in Detroit, the Sixties had ended in flames a full two years prior.

If Detroit was the home of the American Dream, then it would also be the site of confrontation with the American Nightmare. As one of Detroit's most famous sons, Marvin Gaye, once said, "Detroit was heaven, but also hell." The Detroit Rebellion (or Riot) of 1967 was one of the most decisive events in Motor City history, reflecting the racial injustices at the core of American society. After a raid on an after-hours speakeasy, disgruntled residents took to the streets to channel their pent-up frustration into physical actions. The expression of this rage took the form of looted businesses and four hundred destroyed buildings. In the morning, flames decimated the city as ominous dark smoke streaked the skyline. But in order to understand what happened, we need to go back much further in the city's history. The underlying causes of the riot were fueled by racial discrimination after World War II, industrial disinvestment between 1948 and '63, and unfettered residential segregation on the basis of race. Whether it was ordinary whites or real-estate brokers, the game had been rigged against African Americans moving into the city for decades, and the rebellion can be seen as a response to pent-up feelings of rage at the injustices that were continuing to occur.

What happened in Detroit sent shockwaves across the country, galvanizing a push in the Civil Rights Movement.

The folk singer Gordon Lightfoot put the feeling around the rebellion into the lyrics of his song "Black Day in July," singing:

Motor City madness has touched the countryside
And through the smoke and cinders
You can hear it far and wide.

When Martin Luther King Jr. was assassinated a few weeks later, the song was pulled from the airwaves. In the final reckoning, there were nearly 7,500 arrests and forty-three dead. The resulting damage was amongst the worst in American history, until it was surpassed by the Los Angeles Riots of 1992. Lightfoot sums up the aftermath:

In the streets of Motor City there's a deadly silent sound
And the body of a dead youth lies stretched upon the ground
Upon the filthy pavements no reason can be found

Though poignant, Lightfoot's tune, a misty-eyed sing-along, does not correctly capture the feverish musical response to the riot. To better understand the incendiary spirit coursing through Detroit's veins after the rebellion, it makes more sense to look to the city's musicians themselves, who responded by creating the musical equivalents to a blazing mutiny. Motown responded with a slew of psychedelic-soul records, whereas garage rockers turbocharged their sound, effectively birthing punk rock a decade before it would officially take shape at New York City's CBGB club.

Unlike Los Angeles, Detroit would never fully recover from the traumatic reality-rupture caused by the riots. When the Sixties died in Detroit, it was more than hippy life that disappeared. White flight accelerated, unionized jobs began to cave in under pressure and the tell-tale signs of de-industrialization began. The empire was ending. This was an undeniable turning point and a human tragedy on a mass scale. More than hippy paranoia on Hermosa Beach, we're talking about a moment when promises were captured, when dreams turned to nightmares and the lights of the city began receding. But when the factory lights began flickering, a revolutionary group of artists, musicians and activists turned on the emergency power supply. The result was an efflorescence of radical creativity.

Hidden Music at the Hideout

Though Detroit garage rock had been well-established as a popular music styling before the city's riots — as we'll see — it took on a particularly incendiary brand after. We can perhaps best pinpoint the origin of face-melting Detroit garage rock with the B-side of the Pleasure Seekers' 1965 single "Never Thought You'd Leave Me," a little number called "What A Way to Die."

Coming from Grosse Pointe, the all-girl group was fronted by lead singing sisters Suzi and Patti Quatro. After forming the band, they would regularly rock the fledgling teen club, the Hideout, alongside future Detroit stars Bob Seger and Ted Nugent. Their electric shows at the Hideout resulted in a growing reputation as one of the finest bands in Detroit. "What A Way to Die" finds the Pleasure Seekers sowing the seeds of punk with ramshackle production, while Suzi howls about dying from teenage alcoholism. The badass tune finds Suzi sipping on an iced cold bottle of Detroit-made beer Strohs. She hollers, "I may not live past 21, but what a way to die!" From the beginning, Detroit garage rock had a preoccupation with walking the line between life and death, all at the expense of ecstatic excess and possessed pleasures.

When the Pleasure Seekers disbanded, Suzi Quatro would continue on a successful solo career, releasing her self-titled solo debut in 1973. Moreover, Quatro's attitude and leadership over her all-male backing band projected an image of a newly empowered woman that many female listeners found inspiring. Her attitude was infectious, which music journalist Philip Norman described as "a tomboy, lank-haired, tight-bottomed and (twice) tattooed; a rocker, a brooder, a loner, a knife-carrier; a hell-cat, a wild cat, a storm child, refugee from the frightened city of Detroit." As it would turn out, Quatro was just the beginning.

Motor City is Burning

You know the Motor City is burning, people
There ain't a thing about it they can do
My hometown burning down to the ground
Worse than Vietnam

MC5, "Motor City is Burning"

While Motown was going through a psychedelic rebirth, Detroit garage rockers were undergoing both a sonic and ideological radicalization of their own. At the forefront of these insurgent changes were a group called the Motor City 5, or MC5.

MC5 stood out amongst their peers thanks to their electrifying, preaching vocalist Rob Tyner and the dual guitar attack of Wayne Kramer and Fred "Sonic" Smith. Between songs, Tyner would deliver revolutionary sermons damning the ruling class and segregationists while the twin-guitarists were on standby, ready to unleash blistering riffs and mutilating waves of feedback. The group's interest in feedback came from Kramer's love of free-jazz musicians like John Coltrane and Albert Ayler. Solidifying the group's connections to radical politics was their manager John Sinclair, a titanic figure in Michigan countercultural history.

Splintering off from the radical art collective the Detroit

Artists' Workshop out of Wayne State University, the White Panther Party was formed by John Sinclair, Leni Sinclair and Pun Plamondon. Central to the party's ideology was anti-racism and anti-capitalism. First and foremost, the group advocated for the legalization of marijuana, for which John had been arrested several times. Additionally, both John and Leni were heavily associated with the area's musical scenes. While John would manage MC5, Leni became a leading rock photographer — her iconic stills immortalizing everyone from Iggy Pop to Prince.

Indeed, while the White Panthers' mission statement could be summed up — according to Sinclair in a 2021 interview with Jacobin — as "rock 'n roll, dope, sex in the streets and the abolishing of capitalism," it was a much more serious proposition than some dorm-room hippies pontificating about the "man" and "system." These were revolutionaries with a rock-solid ideological roadmap doing actual organizing and activist work. The solidity of this ideology is illustrated in their Ten-Point Plan, adapted from the Black Panther Party, whom they looked up to as heroes. Putting their ideology into praxis, the White Panther Party — according to Sinclair again — also "set up food co-ops, data centers and voter registration drives." As a result of these initiatives, they were able to successfully "elect people to the city council and pass laws that were beneficial to the people, like a free clinic, free daycare center, free school, free food, free this and free that." Operating in Detroit but also out of the nearby college town and countercultural hub Ann Arbor, the White Panthers were able to usher in a golden age in southeastern Michigan. There's also little doubt that their influence has rippled out into the present and is in no small part a reason why Ann Arbor is famously lax on marijuana. The White Panthers firmly took a stance on the Detroit Rebellion, asserting that the riots were justified due to the police brutality and the political and economic conditions of the city at the time. Later, to avoid misinterpreted associations with White Power organizations, the party renamed itself the Rainbow People's Party to avoid false accusations of dog-whistling.

This is a part of the heady social and political milieu that MC5 not just inhabited but were central to. The group, determined to challenge all pre-conceived ideas and taboos, is famous for one of the great moments of rock 'n roll obscenity. Instead of recording a proper debut LP, the band decided to release, in 1969, *Kick Out the Jams*, a live record that captured both the feverish energy of their live show and the radical politics between songs. After they finish the opening number, a furious rendition of "Ramblin' Rose," a gasping-for-air Tyner addresses the crowd. "Right now," he chokes out, "Right now it's time to..." a moment of anticipation and, "...kick out the jams, motherfucker!" With that the band delivers an explosive performance of "Kick Out the Jams," one of the highest energy rock songs of the Sixties. These days, when profanity is so widely used in popular music, it's difficult to imagine the controversy such language could spark. As a result, some stores removed the album, but the incident had little overall impact. Due to their relentless gigging and infectious live shows — that often left fans in a state of exhaustion and ecstasy — the group had amassed popularity and therefore interest from big labels. By 1969, they were riding high, appearing on the cover of *Rolling Stone*.

One of the great instances of total digital recall — the phenomenon of being able to dial up any past experience via the internet — is a 1970 MC5 performance at Tartar Field at Wayne State University on the TV program *Detroit Tube Works*. It's here that some sense of the kinetic power the band channeled is best captured. The footage is a total revelation, with the group's performance additionally heightened perhaps by playing in their hometown. Their rendition of "Looking at You" from this performance is particularly striking. It's a ferocious tune built on a mere two chords, carried by pure energy and a one-of-a-kind bass line from Michael Davis, while Kramer and Smith demonstrate some of the most virtuosic shredding of the period. Adding to the impact, the guitarists sync up their playing with some brilliantly timed moves. Filtered through the static, the performance genuinely sounds on the verge of blowing out the speakers. Most interestingly of all though, from the perspective of 2022, the performance is as instructive as it is enjoyable in watching the bewildered and shocked crowd. It's this that helps to give MC5, some fifty years in all manner of innovations in attack and volume later, the immediate context they need to be understood, the stunned and hypnotized spectators taken aback by the sheer force of their sound.

The legacy of MC5 is massively important in terms of fusing the musical with the political, and it is no surprise to learn that they would become one of the key influences of the anti-establishment punk movement. Furthermore, as we'll see in a moment, MC5's web of influence sprawled out to incorporate a group of anarchic misfits that would elevate rock music to new extremes. One of these, formed in the aftermath of MC5 and the Stooges, was a Detroit supergroup formed by MC5 guitarist Fred "Sonic" Smith — the short-lived, dynamite Sonic's Rendezvous Band. One of the great groups in all of rock history, the SRB featured the Stooges' Scott "Rock Action" Asheton, the Rationals' Scott Morgan and neglected Detroit band Up's Gary Rasmussen. The formation of the band reflected not just the garage scene's intertwining network and mutual support, but one of the key motifs of Detroit's music scene across all genres — freewheeling collective energy and cross-genre experimentation. The SRB was a true tour de force and their best-known song, the rip-roaring "City Slang," is an ode to Detroit itself.

This urge to interact and experiment sonically is also there in two of the groups that spun off MC5's legacy, pushing proto-punk even closer to punk itself — Death and Destroy All Monsters. Both had been neglected until recent reassessments and reissues have helped bring Detroit back to the forefront of the punk and hardcore scenes where it belongs.

The origin of punk rock is usually located in New York City at the CBGB's club with bands like Suicide, the Ramones, the Dead Boys, Patti Smith, Television and more circa 1975. Contrary to that received wisdom, punk rock *really* began two years prior when a trio of black brothers from Detroit started playing speedy, political, power-chord driven rock in 1973. The Hackney brothers — Bobby, David and Dannis — never called their music "punk," because the movement that it became associated with didn't yet exist. Rather, the guys just thought of their music as descending from the rich lineage of ramshackle, rust-belt rock 'n roll.

Black guys picking up guitars and playing fiery on-point garage and punk has itself a storied history in Detroit. We'll explore that lineage more fully later, but Death were the progenitors of a number of things both locally and nationally. In an attempt to rewrite the record, Death's punk rock pioneering became the subject of the 2012 documentary by Mark Christopher Covino and Jeff Howlett, *A Band Called Death*. Finally, with the racial reckoning and consciousness-raising that came with Black Lives Matter protests in the summer of 2020, a widespread awareness of Death's trailblazing place in musical history has started to crystallize, thanks to social media info banners crediting black artists with the birthing of almost every important genre of the twentieth century.

In an interview conducted with the band by Cornelius

"The Reel Hustler" Gross, vocalist and bassist Bobby Hackney explained the origin of their name, commenting:

> Death is the door. We can't take the name the Doors because that's already taken, but [David] was very convinced that Jim Morrison had that same concept. He said look at the lyrics, "break on through to the other side." Where's the other side? He's talking about going through the doors.

If the Doors opened portals to new worlds in moments of drug-fueled reverie, it's Detroit's Death, way ahead of the curve, at the post-Fordist futures' bleeding and crumbling edge, who represent the jump through the doors of perception and into the Real beyond.

Punk isn't the only trajectory that MC5's blown-out rock excess and the Stooges' untamed garage shamanism leads to, though. Destroy All Monsters was an avant-garde rock band composed of University of Michigan art students. It was fronted by scene queen Niagara, who went on to become a successful visual artist. Their early gigs, impromptu performances at frat houses in Ann Arbor, would ruffle feathers with their experimental use of non-instruments. Legendary critic of the day Lester Bangs, from the iconic Detroit rock magazine *CREEM*, was on the scene, characterizing the band as "anti-rock," while Sonic Youth's Thurston Moore credits the group as the first true noise band. Niagara's performance style was unorthodox and distinctive, earning her band a growing reputation and again, in testimony to Detroit's restless and supportive spirit, the group became a proper Detroit supergroup when she enlisted legendary local personnel in the form of MC5 bassist Michael Davis and the Stooges' Ron Asheton.

Destroy All Monsters' defining track is "Bored," also their first proper recording. The notion of boredom is an important one and, it might be argued, the central impetus for all cultural production in and of itself. It is at least an integral experience for the generation that was key in the formation of punk rock. In our contemporary high-speed world of phones constantly keeping us in a distracted state, no one's ever bored in the traditional sense; yet, as Mark Fisher remarked, everything is boring. For example, when lining up to wait for one's turn, we can pass the time scrolling or catching up on the constant bombardment of communications coming at us; indeed, we might even feel in some sense compelled to do so. Under these circumstances of smartphone ubiquity and "digital twitch," we start to yearn for what I'll call *Boredom 1.0* — a time when, rather than feeling the compulsive instinct to check our devices, we might have to simply wait unassisted and unpalliated, giving ourselves up instead to the internal processes that spawn moments of self-reflection or daydreams that can lead off in all kinds of unchosen directions. The mind has no choice but to wander, question and play. When Boredom 1.0 is the underpinning of a culture, when there are few immediately available forms of entertainment beyond one's immediate social field, questioning and play predominate, and you get people — trained musicians or not — coming together to form bands and create art. Indeed, this was the case with Destroy All Monsters, whose first iteration of members couldn't play their instruments when they formed. So, Niagara shouts that she's bored, but boredom, unpressured free time and untethered minds were responsible for some of the great modernist art movements. Perhaps this is central to what ought to be championed in an acid communist antidote to the age of Big Tech tyranny — the generative capacity of boredom and the communal as against entertainment and the social.

But we have jumped forward a few years and now need to loop back to focus on another of Detroit's seminal acts, a band of immeasurable influence and importance in the formation of almost everything of interest that came after them: the Stooges.

Calling from the Fun House

Writing this shortly after my twenty-second birthday, I am listening to the Stooges' track "1969" off their mind-melting self-titled debut record. Fittingly, Iggy Pop sings:

Last year I was twenty-one
I didn't have a lot of fun
and now I'm going to be twenty-two
I say oh my and a boo hoo

Having spent the year in a post-traumatic malaise and looking forward to another series of forthcoming lockdowns, the lyrics resonate a bit too nicely. Yet, what really strikes me is Pop's acquiescence. Released in 1969, Pop sings as though the decade has been dead for years, or as if it never got started in the first place. It makes sense — in Detroit, the aspirations of the Sixties had been suffocated two years prior under the oppressive weight of billowing riot smoke.

Formed in 1967, the same year as the riot, the Stooges spent their gestation years in the college town and countercultural headquarters of Ann Arbor, just a forty-minute drive from Detroit proper. It is reported — from the band themselves — that in these early years the pre-eminent titans of garage rock would get loaded on copious amounts of marijuana, spin freshly scored avant-garde records and sit in the dark all night long envisioning their high thrills, scorching sound. The group's seemingly surprising partiality to the likes of John Cage and Karlheinz Stockhausen — perhaps a product of the restlessness of Boredom 1.0 — established a solid link with experimental (and German) composition that bleeds through into their songs and production values. With this in mind, it's perhaps no surprise that later lead vocalist Iggy Pop would flee the States for a city that I'd argue is in some ways psychically twinned with Detroit — the divided mecca of Cold War bohemia, Berlin.

Originally known as the Psychedelic Stooges, the band's dynamite sound was supplied by brothers Ron and Scott Asheton — on guitar and drums respectively — and Dave Alexander on bass. Elevating the scrappy rockers to dangerously high heights was the precocious bandleader James Osterberg on vocals. Despite their conception in Ann Arbor, the Stooges — by all accounts — are a Detroit band. More than that, they are Detroit rock royalty. Shortly after formation, they began actively gigging in the city, playing alongside MC5, who championed them like their little brothers. The Stooges then relocated to Detroit, squatting in a dilapidated house.

The Stooges were the Four Horsemen of the 1960s, sounding the sirens of the decade's death. Released the same week as the Manson murders, the group's explosive self-titled 1969 debut distils everything radical about 1960s music into a concise slice of no-frills rock 'n roll. Produced by the legendary (Velvet) Underground musician John Cale, the record is — on the whole — anything but stereotypical of the period. The A-side, just three tracks, is amongst the most forward-thinking side of vinyl the decade ever produced. Signaling the end of an era, the apocalyptic opener "1969" rings out like gunshots, shot through with blasts of fuzzy wah-wah riffs and crushing walls of sound. That takes the listener into one of the most important tracks in punk history, "I Wanna Be Your Dog." Anchored by a dark, descending three-chord run, the track is a foray into the kinky world of Osterberg, who had by now transformed himself into the menacing, jeering Iggy Pop.

As a testament to its legacy, the tune is amongst the most regularly covered songs by Detroit bands, and punk groups at large. Rather than keep the onslaught of heart-stopping rock going, the album then pivots to the ten-minute chant-dirge "We Will Fall." It's here that the group's secret love for avant-garde reveals itself most clearly. It sounds like something out of a death cult ritual where sacrifice is imminent. This is also where Cale's influence shows itself most clearly. With unsettling droning strings reminiscent of the Velvet's "Venus in Furs," Cale's background role as producer briefly moves to the forefront of the album. Despite this ingenuity, the notoriously stuffy rock-critic Robert Christgau deemed the record "stupid-rock at its best." But there's nothing dumb about the Stooges' debut effort. Quite the opposite — their intelligence lies precisely in their unparalleled ability to distil both experimentalist abstraction and garage's libidinal energy into a slab of left-field, avant-punk perfection. All in all, the record is aptly self-titled, as it captures everything the group was about.

Just when listeners thought rock music had reached its limit, the Stooges returned a year later with their magnum opus, 1970's *Fun House* — a record that marks the shift into the new decade better than any other release. With trippy album artwork that appears to depict their self-destructive bandleader Iggy Pop engulfed in flames, *Fun House* is the sound of a city burning to the ground. Like a lit match dropping on a pool of oil, "Down on the Street" opens the record with Ron Asheton's guitar sliding into a chugging fury. Over this, Pop howls like a laughing hyena, plunging us into the Stooges' alternate universe, the Fun House, with its distorting halls of mirrors, mysterious dayglo signs and symbols, dead ends and hidden chambers, a thrilling, disorienting space of transcendence and old-time carny madness. There has been nothing like it before or since. In his book *Ghosts of My Life*, Mark Fisher notes:

The slow cancellation of the future has been accompanied by a deflation of expectations. There can be few who believe that in the coming year a record as great as, say, the Stooges' *Fun House* [...] will be released.

For Fisher, Detroit is always there as a reminder of what is possible and what has been lost.

But beyond Fisher holding the record up as a pillar of musical innovation, the simplicity of Pop's lyricism on *Fun House,* with tracks marked by urgent repetitions and chants, helps to elaborate one of the themes that has been teased out of his acid communism: *exorbitant sufficiency.* Author Carl Neville — who was in discussion with Fisher at the inception of acid communism — notes in a blog post that the defining feature of what Fisher terms exorbitant sufficiency, in reference to the semi-hallucinatory euphoria experienced by the British DJ Danny Baker on a family holiday, is "time, free or unpressured time, and the sense of unpressured time comes from both Baker having been a child at the time, but also from a lack of anxiety about the future." This idea — the ability to luxuriate in free time, anxiety-free, as if tomorrow doesn't exist — permeates *Fun House*. Further, Fisher argued elsewhere that this was the great generational experience of the Fordist period: a sense of time opening up, the work week reducing, the weekend and leisure taking on a central role in life; secure jobs and readily affordable accommodation widely available. Taken together, these conditions then allow for the rootedness that builds social relations as well as the ability to live relatively carefree, non-competitive lives that are in marked contrast to the insecurity, expense precarity, relentless competition and unproductive boredom and anxiety that characterize the post-Fordist world.

Perhaps the clearest example of the Stooges' own

euphoric, exorbitantly sufficient epiphany is on "1970." Opening the track, Iggy yelps:

Out of my mind on a Saturday night
1970 rollin' in sight

Immediately, we are firmly placed in the present moment while the future is rushing benignly in like a great warm wave. We're also dropped into a Saturday night when the pressures and stressors of the work week are behind us. Reaching an intense repetition, vamping on the same chords over and over again, "1970" climaxes with Iggy passionately repeating *ad infinitum*, "I feel alright!" While "I feel alright" will strike Christgau no doubt as more dumb rock, in some senses the ability to utter this phrase is at the burning core of what acid communism strives for. A feeling of contentment with one's place in the world so great that it overflows the moment and bathes everything in its glow. Baker's incredulous "this is happening now," the phrase he repeats to himself in the *Acid Communism* introduction, and Pop either feeling so good because he's tripping or tripping because he's feeling so good as he watches the future arrive, share a common root, psychedelicizing one's relationship to labor, leisure, love and time and transforming the mundane, a Saturday night, a family holiday, into the extraordinary. This is the promise of acid communism, which we might also think of as a collective entering of the Fun House — not just the ability to say it, but to find oneself involuntarily repeating, again and again, "I feel alright," amazed to discover that it cannot be said enough or that the feeling cannot be exhausted.

Fun House comes from the future. Like a hyperdense object shot through musical space-time, the record's influence is felt everywhere, germinating in krautrock bands like Neu! and Can — who were no doubt inspired by its oddly repetitive but also freeform nature — creating the endless motorik loop as part of a wider European trajectory that mutates into the trailblazing synthesizer work of Kraftwerk and Giorgio Moroder, who provided the new sonic conditions that would make disco possible. *Fun House* would also return from the future in the form of disco's time-extending 12" singles and theme of radical self-love. Like the Stooges, disco wasn't about feeling loved by others, but the insistence that — as Donna Summer tells us again and again in Moroder's towering signature work — "*I* feel love." It isn't that Summer feels love for anyone in particular or is loved by another; the love she feels may, ambiguously, be coming either from within her in an objectless outpouring of sheer delight or something she is absorbing from the blissed-out atmosphere around her. *I* feel alright, *I* feel love. On the disco dance-floor, one can dance with others, but also turn inwards and endlessly dance with oneself. Like Iggy, the key here is a sense of autonomy and self-sufficiency.

The Fun House, like the Temptations' Psychedelic Shack and Moroder's endlessly dilating emotion-drenched dancefloor, is a space that sits outside of time, a liminal zone. Perhaps we could adapt Hakim Bey's idea of the T.A.Z, (Temporary Autonomous Zone, used to designate a space that, for a moment, evades capitalism's capture and regulation) and christen these time-spaces "Temporary *Atemporal* Zones" — arenas where, for a moment, we are freed from the pasts and futures, both personal and political, that haunt us. As we'll discuss more in the following chapter, when Fisher pointed to Norman Whitfield and the Temptations, perhaps he was really — subconsciously — pointing to Detroit's uniquely scrambled, psychedelic ethos and abundance of liminal zones that take the form of abandoned neighborhoods, factories and eerie overgrowths that are once again reminiscent of the Zone in Tarkovsky's

Stalker. Of course, this is a notion that gets at one of the core themes of this entire book: the music of Detroit has always been animated by a certain understanding that time is out of joint in a uniquely positive way.

Lust for Life

Like the Berlin in which he temporarily made his home, Iggy is also seemingly divided. While there is the exorbitantly sufficient, child-like Iggy, there is also the self-destructive, death-driven Iggy. In Joan Didion's *The White Album*, she describes the music of the Doors as that which "insisted that love was sex and sex was death and therein lay salvation." But if this description applies to any musician, it is surely the Stooges' Iggy Pop. Convulsing his body in a libidinal fury on stage, Pop acted out Didion's description by masochistically self-harming for entertainment, rolling around in shattered glass and stomping his feet to the Asheton brothers' fiery rhythms, all while streaked in his own blood. Simultaneously, he would make disturbing, seductive gestures and expose himself on stage. Iggy Pop — like Didion's example of the Doors' gothic prince Jim Morrison — illustrates the horrifying relationship between love, sex and death. And it is this obscene and transgressive Iggy, the inner-child as maniacal and self-destructive rather than serene and self-absorbed, that we must also explore and account for.

In *The Melancholia of Class*, her brilliant book about both her own experiences and those of working-class artists in general, Cynthia Cruz — writing on Joy Division's Ian Curtis, a figure who was himself influenced by Pop's work and who would later influence another of Detroit's more famous sons, the rapper Danny Brown — notes how "the extreme compression of libidinal energy becomes a death drive. There is no space between life and the music: their lived experience was channeled directly into the music." This certainly applies to Iggy Pop too. In order to see why, we need to go back to the time before he was Iggy Pop and "the Godfather of Punk," when Jim Osterberg was just a young man growing up in a trailer in Ypsilanti.

Osterberg's early experiences in the family home set him up with a degree of security and comfort that perhaps allowed him to work through and survive the pressure that being a working-class artist exerted on his psyche. But despite his parents' encouragement, those wider structural forces could not be sidestepped entirely. Osterberg recalls, for instance, how, showing a deep love and dedication to music, his parents — using the limited space they had — vacated their bedroom to allow Jim to practice on his drumkit. Reflecting on this class-specific experience, Iggy recalled in a 2007 *Rolling Stone* interview:

> Once I hit junior high in Ann Arbor, I began going to school with the son of the president of Ford Motor Company, with kids of wealth and distinction. But I had a wealth that beat them all. I had the tremendous investment my parents made in me. I got a lot of care. They helped me explore anything I was interested in. This culminated in their evacuation from the master bedroom in the trailer, because that was the only room big enough for my drum kit. They gave me their bedroom.

We might consider the impact of such a gracious gesture from Osterberg's parents. To see one's family give up coveted space to allow one to pursue their passion is not to be taken lightly. This moving moment surely lit a certain fire in Pop, a need to succeed and soldier on no matter how hard things got. This urgency is reflected in the intensity of Pop's performances, which oscillate between lust for life and readiness to sacrifice it all, dying on stage. Parental love works as a buffer, but the working-class artist has a set of contradictions that they will have to work through, irrespective of the specifics of their background. Exploring the liminality and overflow of pressure pushed on the working class, Cruz notes that, in most cases, the working-class artist possessed by the death drive will inevitably experience a breaking point. Discussing Ian Curtis and Amy Winehouse, she notes that there is:

> No simulation, no translation, the libidinal energy, internalized, was the same energy utilized for writing lyrics, making music. Such a direct and powerful current, with no means of siphoning off, can only lead to combustion. Winehouse died of a heart attack, resulting from her chronic anorexia, and Curtis of suicide by hanging. The libidinal energy trapped inside their bodies — pulsating, overwhelming — informs every aspect of their lives and, in the end, overcomes them, the death drive, taking over.

This is the flipside of exorbitant sufficiency, the alternate path of the life-current, the darker side of excessive embodiment, the body experienced as a too-muchness rather than a fullness, resulting in extreme acts in the attempt to regulate it, like self-harm and psychosis. Indeed, after cutting powerhouse albums and achieving success, after the exhibitionist performances and drug-fueled pleasures, and after leaving Detroit for the glossy unreality of Los Angeles, the man that called himself Iggy Pop found himself confronting a broken Jim Osterberg. Caught between worlds and plummeting deeper towards rock bottom, Pop too had reached a breaking point. Rather than convulsing on stage, he could be found in the gutters outside of clubs and hiding away in drug bunkers. But unlike Ian

Curtis and Amy Winehouse, Iggy Pop had a friend going through a similar situation who would save him from this darkness.

That friend was fellow working-class artist and frequent collaborator David Bowie, who had worked on producing Iggy & the Stooges seminal 1973 album, *Raw Power*. Interestingly, regaling Bowie with stories of the Detroit Riot, Pop in turn inspired Bowie's track "Panic in Detroit" from his 1973 record *Aladdin Sane*. The great alien messiah, the Starman known as Ziggy Stardust, was also suffering from an overdose of American artificiality and drugs, as could be seen in his 1975 interviews, so coked-out that he had no recollection recording his phenomenal 1976 album *Station to Station*. In some sort of coke-comedown moment of clarity, the by-then emaciated Thin White Duke resolved to get better. Now he needed to find a location for his rehab.

In his Los Angeles bunker, Bowie had been obsessively watching films from the German Expressionism movement, like Fritz Lang's *Metropolis*. Further, he had become obsessed with Kraftwerk, a group so important to the story of Detroit's music that it cannot be understated. Finally, Bowie was tired of the overwhelming newness of Los Angeles. These factors led him to settle in Berlin, a city overflowing with a haunted history of its own. And so, taking Iggy with him, the burned-out glam punks retreated from America and back into history.

In Berlin, the two would create some of their most introspective and futuristic music, with the help of Brian Eno and longtime Bowie producer Tony Visconti. Bowie worked on his haunting Berlin Trilogy — *Low, Heroes* and *Lodger*. Before that, Iggy came up with *The Idiot*, a record whose title was inspired by Dostoevsky's novel of the same name and whose dark and sparse urbanism went on to inspire a whole host of post-punkers.

Perhaps we can begin to see a certain symbiotic

relationship forming between Detroit and Berlin, a sort of portal between these places, two somewhat different but still paradigmatic cities of the postwar period beginning to open. The lineage goes something like this: German avant-garde music inspiring the Stooges, the Stooges inspiring German bands, Bowie and Pop taking cues from Kraftwerk, calling them the future and drawing them in to investigate further. We'll see this call-and-response relationship continue across time and space later when we arrive at the birth of techno.

Searching for Sugar Man: The Eerie Story of Sixto Rodriguez

But before we move on, we'll take a detour into another uncanny doubling and tracking of the ways Detroit's influence reaches out and returns in ghostly form. While Iggy was being received in Berlin and touring around Europe, another, much more unassuming Detroit musician was being lauded elsewhere.

One of the great stories of music underdog history is that of Sixto Diaz Rodriguez. A private individual with an exceptionally humble aura, Rodriguez was an enigmatic Detroit musician in the late Sixties and early Seventies who kept a low profile, churning out folky psych-pop songs. As a young man, Rodriguez attended Detroit's Wayne State University where he received a bachelor's degree in philosophy. If Rodriguez was imbibing grand philosophical ideas, his personal philosophy is one of simplicity, perhaps in line with a thinker like the Ancient Greek Epicurus. After releasing two fantastic records that failed to amass attention — 1970's *Cold Fact* and 1971's *Coming From Reality* — Rodriguez picked up a career in construction and dedicated himself to raising his family. For most musicians who fail to break out of obscurity, this is usually where the story ends. However, for Rodriguez, this is precisely where his story takes an unlikely and unusual turn.

Virtually unknown even in Detroit, Rodriguez assumed his music had been completely forgotten, but unbeknownst to him, his records had successfully made their way to South Africa where his bootlegs were issued on labels and taken up as the soundtrack of South African revolution. Considered a revolutionary songwriter like Pete Seeger or Bob Dylan, Rodriguez became South Africa's best-selling artist, promoting unity, peace and love across the apartheid-torn country. Decades later, fans learned that their exemplary artist was not actually dead — as it had been rumored that he committed suicide shortly after recording *Coming from Reality* — but, on the contrary, very much alive. When fans found this out, he came to South Africa where he played to sold-out stadiums. The story is recounted in the excellently eerie documentary, *Searching for Sugar Man*.

What does the story of Sugar Man tell us? On its surface, it's a bit unsettling to think how far one's influence can extend without ever knowing it, that an artist assumed dead, languishing in obscurity, is fundamental to the lives and struggles of a people thousands of miles away. Rodriguez's story is certainly an example of Detroit's influence reaching other places and then becoming more popular abroad than at home. Like a virus, once Detroit's music spreads outside the city, it begins to infect, influence and take on a life of its own. Though other cities could imitate and build off Detroit's musical exports, none could replicate the conditions that made it possible to create such innovations in the first place: the city's strange generative power to both move the dial politically and yet do so through the production of phantoms.

3. ON CLOUD NINE: MOTOWN'S PSYCHEDELIC SOUL

Acid's information supernova blows up the ego.
Kodwo Eshun, *More Brilliant Than the Sun*

In lieu of the 1967 uprising, Motown responded with a pivot in sound. While the guitar-wielding garage rock bands were birthing punk, Motown groups embraced themes of both psychic and political upheaval. There was something mind-expanding in the air, and the feeling of psychic revolution was flowing across the country.

The first stirrings of this psychedelic sentiment in Motown came from the Supremes. Beginning with a sci-fi synthesizer, their 1967 single "Reflections" finds Diana Ross looking through the mirror of her mind, trapped in a distorted reality, haunted by memories of a lost love. Like Detroit's ubiquitous mementos of a lost future, Ross sees this former flame reflected back everywhere she goes. Through the tears she cries, an uncontrollable hurt surfaces. This is psychedelia as psychological release, a kinetic confrontation with what haunts our psyche. Lurking beneath the surface of consciousness is a gateway, with the potential to both obliterate and liberate us. But ultimately, "Reflections," like Detroit after the uprising, ends in disintegration. "Right before my eyes," Ross croons, "my world has turned to dust." The Supremes predated psychedelic-soul proper once again with their next single, "Love Child." While the hippy counterculture was preoccupied with the child as a symbol of purity and innocence, the Supremes' tune — in a sense

— flips the script. The song's subject, a love child, is born out of wedlock and enters the world as an object of scorn. The song is a slab of psychedelic-pop perfection, and — as women's artistic contributions typically are — has been largely neglected in the story of psychedelic soul.

"Love Child" was released in 1968, the same year that Motown moved offices to the Donovan building, a sleek art-deco structure designed by the epochal architect Albert Kahn, whose glorious structures, like the Fisher Building, can be spotted standing throughout the city today. In a tragic case of local-history erasure and capitalistic cruelty, the Donovan was demolished in 2006 to make more space for Super Bowl parking. The decision was made without much thought, and given the greenlight by crooked mayor Kwame Kilpatrick, who offhandedly called the legendary piece of Motown history "an eyesore." Disappointed Detroiters noted that the speedy demolition meant that important artifacts never made it out of the building. It isn't just Ross's inner world that has turned to dust, but through forgetfulness, cultural vandalism and the desire to constantly remap has also destroyed much of both her storied legacy and that of the city's too.

"Reflections" and "Love Child" represent the emergence of what Emily Lordi has dubbed "black psychedelia," a musical form that engages with a certain earthbound, present-day social realism, while at the same time hinting, through its use of the studio and effects, at the malleability and plasticity of given structures. The contrasts, tensions and overlaps between the definition of black psychedelia and the ideas of Afrofuturism are something we'll explore as we go forward, looking at Fisher's exemplary acid communist band the Temptations and their producer Norman Whitfield. In agreement with Lordi, I'll suggest that black psychedelia emerges as a distinct movement, which can be contrasted with George Clinton's experiments with psychedelic Afrofuturism in Funkadelic, and that Detroit is in many ways the crucible of these two important sounds, genres, perhaps even cosmologies.

There are of course any number of important actors in this emergent black psychedelia and in Motown's pivot toward psychedelic soul, and highlighting any one is liable to leave just as many arguably equally important contributors out, but one undoubtedly central element was the freewheelin' guitar playing of Dennis Coffey. In 1966, Coffey became a new addition to the Funk Brothers, Motown's legendary — and largely unheralded — ensemble of studio musicians. Coffey — a virtuosic player — began to infuse his jazzy stylings with distortion, trippy echo-delays and, most importantly, wah-wah pedals. Mirroring the experience of an acid trip, guitar effects were a way of turning music in on itself. Today, after the mind-blowing innovations of shoegaze groups like Slowdive and My Bloody Valentine, it's hard to conceptualize just how radical these sorts of new guitar sounds were on the ears, but in 1966 they were — and still are with the right kind of ears — capable of producing a dip into distorted reality.

At this same time, a hungry-for-success Motown upstart was eager to prove himself. When Motown's powerhouse songwriting trio Holland/Dozier/Holland quit due to unfair payment by Gordy, the ambitious Norman Whitfield — a man who had been waiting in the wings for years — stepped in. Determined to prove himself when he had three pairs of big shoes to fill, Whitfield pushed for the release of one of his 1966 compositions, meaning that 1967 saw Whitfield producing a tune he had written the year prior, Motown's biggest hit yet, Marvin Gaye's number one "I Heard it Through the Grapevine." Initially rejected by Gordy, "Grapevine" was finally released in 1968 and spent more time than any other Motown tune at the top of the charts. It was a song about rumors of a lover who has been unfaithful, and the emotional toll they take on the song's protagonist. But released against the backdrop of Vietnam, the grapevine also hints at political hearsays. Stories of protestors attacked, the CIA's involvement in MLK Jr.'s assassination and young men dying in Vietnamese jungles were all being heard about through America's grapevine, whispered about at dive bars, garage rock gigs and on the frontlines of protests. Watching the horrors of Vietnam broadcast on television was to step into the consensual hallucination, a sort of mass-mediated trip that was stranger than fiction. Whitfield — who had mind-expanding psychedelia on the horizon — was giving the country a sort of acid-testing ground with Gaye's palatable croon. With drums like rolling thunder, a sinister organ groove and icy strings, the song's lowkey groove is addicting. As the song's lyrics suggest, the realities of the situation were enough to make a man cry or lose his mind. In 1970, Whitfield would produce another influential political single, Edwin Starr's "War." The track was the fifth most popular song of the year, and a fiery condemnation of the conflict in Vietnam. Unsurprisingly, Armed Forces Radio banned the song so soldiers couldn't hear it.

In his classic book on Afrofuturism and other black diasporic musical trajectories, *More Brilliant Than the Sun*, Kodwo Eshun writes that "Acid opens a cataclysmic continuum between Vietnam, Detroit, and Other Planes out there." Indeed, Detroit was a lab for political consciousness-raising, and it was using Motown's libidinal-pop formula as a way of going overground, effectively bringing radical ideas to the masses. Motown's connections to politics had been present beneath the pop sheen for longer than many may realize. For example, Gordy had been holding on to the rights of a 1963 MLK Jr. speech. Capitalizing on the moment, he began a new division of Motown called the Black Forum Label, which issued a series of Civil Rightsthemed records including speeches by Langston Hughes, Stokely Carmichael and MLK Jr. The release of King's "Why I Oppose the War on Vietnam" coincided with a growing intensity in anti-'Nam sentiment. Now, with the help of Whitfield, Motown would not only embrace political change, but a psychic revolution of almost inconceivable magnitude.

It had taken time, but Whitfield had proven he was more than competent, and next would strut into the realm of artistic giants. Ushering in the era of psychedelic soul, Whitfield began to experiment with the time-tested formula of Fordist ready-made hits when he teamed up with the Temptations. When the group's de facto leader at the time, Otis Williams, tried to persuade Whitfield to go in a darker, more hallucinatory direction, he had some reservations. However, as Fisher notes, "his eventual conversion would lead to some of the most stunning productions in popular music history." The template had been Sly & the Family Stone's "Dance to the Music," a tune that found Sly's motley crew all getting in on vocal duties. The track is a democratization of the mic, capturing a participatory music-making experience in the moment. Using the Family Stone as a starting point, Whitfield would next take inspiration from psychedelic rock, enlisting Coffey as the Detroit equivalent of Hendrix. Finally, adding a final dash of influence from James Brown's electric-funk energy, the new sound of Motown was ready for the acid-testing grounds. Like Brian Wilson on the West Coast and George Martin across the Atlantic, these new recordings showcased Whitfield leaning into using the studio as instrument and laboratory for creativity.

Whitfield was specifically concerned with time itself, and how it could be extended outwards and integrated into the thousand plateaus of life. It was no longer a matter of what a pop song is, or what a pop song has historically represented, but rather, what can a pop song *do*? What radical — but also libidinal — sentiment can be beamed through the airwaves to the masses? What dreamings can we inspire? Through sound, can we evoke new ways of living, loving and experiencing? The notion was to challenge the ideal form of a pop song — which Motown had arguably come closest to producing — and explore what other lines of flight might lay beneath the surface. At the same time, in the world of communications studies, Marshall McLuhan's formulation that the medium *is* the message suggested that there was something inherently powerful within the flows, distributions and waxy grooves of vinyl records themselves. If the messages at protests weren't being broadcast, might messages more efficiently be sent through song? This is what Whitfield and the Temptations dared to find out.

All of these changing tides culminated in the release of the Temptations' groundbreaking 1969 long-player *Cloud Nine*, the first album to win Motown a Grammy. Opening the record with Coffey's psychocandy guitar riffage and drummer Spyder Webb's propulsive double-time rhythm, the titular track whisks us away to a land high in the sky. Writing on the tune "Cloud Nine," Fisher argues that the track has a powerful universal appeal due to its number of interpretations, and thus applicability to varying strategies for revolution:

Sure, you can be what you want to be, but only by being a million miles from reality, only by leaving behind all your responsibilities. This super-egoic appeal could have been endorsed by conservatives as well as a certain brand of radical: conservatives, who wanted everyone to knuckle down to work; militants, who demanded commitment to revolution, which — they said — entailed an attention to the horrors of the world, not a quick fix flight from the real.

Cloud Nine also features the nearly ten-minute-long delirious adventure "Runaway Child, Running Wild." As the title suggests, the song is about a runaway "roaming through the city going nowhere fast." It also gives us an update on the state of Detroit when the group sings of the dark and deserted streets, marrying the sonic experimentation and social commentary that black psychedelia has sought to synthesize into radical new forms. Always a prolific group, they would follow *Cloud Nine*'s heady trip with the more directly politically infused psych-soul staple *Puzzle People* that same year. In contrast with *Cloud Nine*, this new record embraced sentiments of black pride and working-class solidarity, something that can directly be heard and observed on tracks like the Civil Rights commentary "Message from a Black Man" and mass-incarceration critique "Slave." By this point, the group was in full psychedelic-soul swing, and were on the precipice of composing their *magnum opus*.

Psychedelic Shack, That's Where It's At

In 1970, Whitfield and the Temptations released *Psychedelic Shack*, an LP which encapsulates the vision of an acid communism better than any other release of the day. The record is most notable for its lead single, "Psychedelic Shack," which is the Temptations' most fully realized vision of a world which could be free. The song details the experience of spending the night at what seems to be a sort of club, which brings people from all walks of life together. Featuring a rip-roaring performance from the Funk Brothers, Coffey's guitar surges with a squelching wah-wah while the multi-tracked drums lock listeners into a hypnotic groove. On the vocal front, the Temptations are decidedly collective, with each member taking stabs at lead vocal runs. Even relative newcomer Dennis Edwards has isolated lines. In terms of production, Whitfield is at the peak of his powers with a mix that distils all of these elements into a slim single clocking in at just under four minutes.

Writing on the track in *Acid Communism*, Fisher says that:

> "Psychedelic Shack" describes a space that is very definitely collective, that bustles with all the energy of a bazaar. For all its carnivalesque departures from everyday reality, however, this is no remote utopia. It feels like an actual social space, one you can imagine really existing. You are as likely to come upon a crank or a huckster as a poet or musician here, and who knows if today's crank might turn out to be tomorrow's genius? It is also an egalitarian and democratic space, and a certain affect presides over everything. There is multiplicity, but little sign of resentment or malice. It is a space for fellowship, for meeting and talking as much for having your mind blown. If "there's no such thing as time" — because the lighting suspends the distinction between day and night; because drugs affect time-perception — then you are not prey to the urgencies which make so much of workaday life a drudge. There is no limit to how long conversations can last, and no telling where encounters might lead. You are free to leave your street identity behind, you can transform yourself according to your desires, according to desires which you didn't know you had.

Psychedelic Shack. Putting these words in combination provokes all kinds of imaginative possibilities and teasing paradoxes. The psychedelic refers to something transcendent and other-worldly. Meanwhile, a shack might connote poverty, or something cobbled together by a group of friends in a backyard. But given the scale of Motown's success and Detroit's ascendancy in the Fordist world-order, why not envisage a luxury communist psychedelic palace? Perhaps there is something pre-figurative, anticipatory in the Temptations turn to the shack. By 1969, the utopian dreams embedded within Detroit's psychic — and physical — architecture had already begun to dissipate. Not only that, as the Temps sing on "I Can't Get Next to You," from 1969's landmark psych-soul record *Puzzle People*, "I can build a castle from a single grain of sand." The notion is one of making do with what one has and transforming the minimal into the maximal with communal power. The trip was ending, and the Temptations understood that, by using a certain sort of "psychedelic reason", the ordinary could be transformed into the luminary. For Mark Fisher, "psychedelic reason" is the process by which one gets out *through* their head, rather than getting out of their head. In our heads, we can hold onto and live in the pleasure palace forever. The forces of capital might be beyond control, but who's to say our minds have been colonized? The Psychedelic Shack exists on the outer limits, but once inside everything changes.

In the song, the group informs us that the Psychedelic Shack is a place where there is no time, at least not anymore. Conversations can go on forever, there's no point when dancing has to stop. This is mirrored in Whitfield's ever-expanding, time-stretching compositions, which predated the 12" dance singles that were made to keep people on the floor and in their heads. As Fisher informs us in *Acid Communism*:

Whitfield became so entranced by the psychedelic soundscapes he worked on in the studio that he would push for the Temptations to release tracks that were eight or nine minutes long, with space for extended instrumental passages.

In the psychedelic shack, all bets are off. Strobe lights are flashing, producing a glitchy delay in perceptions of movement and, as a result, time itself. Lost in the feedback loops, we no longer function in a linear fashion. There is also an undeniable love in this space; a love that is no longer confined to a couple — to whom the Temptations had written peans like "My Girl" or "The Way You Do the Things You Do," just a few years prior. Instead, the love of the Psychedelic Shack is opened up to a larger, encompassing sense of collectivity.

That same year, the Supremes released *New Ways but Love Stays*, the title of which captures in its most condensed formulation, almost as a slogan, Fisher's formulation that "a new humanity, a new seeing, a new thinking, a new loving: this is the promise of acid communism." New ways, but the love stays. The record featured the single "Stoned Love," a psychedelic ode to achieving unity via a stoned sense of loving others. Reminiscent of Iggy Pop on "Down on the Street," there are "no walls" and no time here, just a love that pervades — a sort of hazy, hallucinatory love that transcends hatred, destruction, and death itself as a way of building new futures.

Though the Psychedelic Shack is a distinctly Detroit phenomenon, its rhizomatic influence took root across the world, forming a number of different iterations. Indeed, we might note that David Mancuso's loft in New York City circa 1970 was one such psychedelic shack, which spiraled out, informing the city's iconic club culture. Another was the Paradise Garage where Larry Levan — a master DJ that would help inspire Detroit techno — would spin euphoric all-night DJ sets throughout the 1980s. Shacks, lofts, garages, these are the spaces in and around the main house, the structures, extensions and antechambers where a new form of living and new desires will be incubated.

Only Love Can Conquer Hate

Simultaneously, all the while, the man who initially teamed up with Whitfield for "I Heard It Through the Grapevine" had his own call-to-arms album percolating.

Marvin Gaye had been a rebel in Motown from the beginning, pushing back against Gordy's insistence on pop hits, opting for his debut to pay tribute to jazzy crooners like Sinatra. Going as far back as 1965 — when he became aware of the Watts Riot — Gaye had been battling with Berry Gordy over permission to release songs speaking out against injustice. His chance came with the unexpected release of the 1971 single "What's Going On." The composition was passed to Gaye by Obie Benson of the Four Tops. Gaye then recorded the tune in a laid-back, communal atmosphere that welcomed new players, improvisation and collaboration. Gordy pushed back against the tune's release, fearing it would not sell, but forces behind the scenes at Motown were so certain of the song's importance that — to both Gaye and Gordy's surprise — the song hit shelves. Immediately proving Gordy wrong, the single was a bestseller. Gaye had proved his vision would both sell and speak to listeners, and now he set out to finish the job. With the release of his legendary 1971 record, *What's Going On*, he would deliver to the world the most concise, sublimely beautiful record of resistance ever put to wax.

Like the Temps' *Psychedelic Shack* and *Puzzle People*, Gaye's *What's Going On* opens with the sounds of conversation in a joyous, communal party space. Placing us within a psychedelic shack of his own, Gaye's masterpiece begins with Eli Fontaine's iconic improvised sax line and a laid-back bass groove. The opening number asks the fundamental question the record sets out to explore: what's *really* going on? Why are Civil Rights leaders all being killed? In a matter of five years, Gaye had witnessed the assassinations of Malcom X, Martin Luther King Jr. and Fred Hampton. What was happening to the industrial cities? How could people thrive under a broken economic system? "Natural fact is, I can't pay my taxes." What was going on at protests? "Picket lines, picket signs, don't punish me with brutality." Why were peaceful students on the frontlines left in tears, maced, beaten to the ground and even killed? "Trigger-happy policing, panic is spreading, God knows where we're heading." Where did all the blue skies go? Who really cares?

Gaye's scope was massive, as he simultaneously sought to make sense of both the larger world-historical and his own personal psychological turmoil. His beloved singing partner Tammi Terrell — with whom he had conquered the highest mountains and widest rivers — had passed away of a malignant tumor the year prior. Attempting to cope with this immense hurt, Gaye was also battling a nasty addiction that brought on even more distress, which was put to song on "Flying High (In the Friendly Sky)." "I go to the place where good feelin' awaits me, self-destruction's in my hand." He saw years ahead of his time, foreshadowing the environmental concerns on the horizon on "Mercy Mercy Me": "Oil wasted on the oceans and upon our seas, fish full of Mercury."

Recorded with copious amounts of Scotch and moral support in the studio, *What's Going On* was finally complete. After channeling years of pent-up rage, distress and trauma into new songs, Gaye's masterpiece was released. For all its immense political and existential questions, Gaye arrives at a simple thesis: *Only love can conquer hate*. It was a swan song to Civil Rights-era optimism and Motown's time in Detroit, but it was also a new beginning for Gaye, ushering in the artistic peak of his career with 1973's *Let's Get It On* and 1976's *I Want You*. His personal swan song, *Midnight Love*, wouldn't come for another decade.

Stepping Into Tomorrow

Another development in psychedelic soul occurred in 1975 when Donald Byrd — a Detroit trumpeter mentioned at the very beginning of this book — released the double-shot of albums *Stepping Into Tomorrow* and *Places and Spaces*. Byrd was raised in Detroit and would receive his undergraduate degree from the city's Wayne State University. After earning his bachelor's, he would leave Michigan and go on to get his Master's at the Manhattan School of Music. Linking up with players in the New York City scene, Byrd would solidify himself as one of the most reliable session musicians of his time and a remarkable band leader in his own right.

Byrd was riding high, but then, in 1973, something very strange happened. That year he released the record that tore up the jazz rulebook and caused a legendarily critical uproar — *Black Byrd*. By enlisting new musicians and infusing jazz with elements of funk, soul and rock, Byrd broke through with a new, psychedelic style that was also, crucially, danceable. Of course, for jazz purists, this new sound was totally taboo, a bastardization of jazz to be squarely rejected by any serious aficionado. Ironically though, the album was in large part responsible for saving Byrd's label, the historic Blue Note Records. Despite the criticisms of *Black Byrd*, Byrd knew he was onto something. Picking up on how all of these strains of black popular music could be elegantly fused together, he arrived in 1975 with the one-two hook that would elevate and reassert the relevance of psychedelic soul music.

Perhaps his 1975 records were Byrd's return to a Detroit state of mind, where genre doesn't fit into confined boxes, but rather exists in a playful exchange with all of the other sweet sounds the city has on offer. Beginning with the titular track, *Stepping Into Tomorrow* is a heady foray into psych-jazz jamming. The opening number's incessant chant returns us to the psychedelic shack's Temporary Atemporal Zone, as Byrd simultaneously grounds us in the present and walks us into the ever-unfolding future. On "Think Twice," Byrd ingeniously fuses smooth soul, raspy funk vocals, easy-listening instrumental breaks and pop hooks into an unforgettable tune that Detroit producer J Dilla — who we'll discuss in chapter six — would cover on his *Welcome 2 Detroit* album.

Then Byrd did it again with *Places and Spaces* that same year. Like the very first sounds of *Psychedelic Shack* and *What's Going On*, the record's opening number "Change (Makes You Want to Hustle)" begins with the sounds of a social gathering where people are hooting and hollering, joyously clapping and shouting "Yeah!" One of the great dance jams of the 1970s, the song combines the libidinal, the pleasureful and the fun with a sense of the philosophical and political. Everything is fluid, and here the ever-changing, always dilating dimensions of daily life, political futures, and time itself are to be approached head on. Meanwhile, "(Fallin' Like) Dominoes," anchored by a wicked funk groove in its verses, cascades into an elegant chorus that reminds us of how physically comforting each other — a studied strategy for healing trauma — can breakdown the crushing weight of the past, allowing our problems to fall away one by one. Indeed, the record is concerned with the "places and spaces out there," but as Byrd seems to realize, the most far-out places are accessed by going deep inside oneself, and using what we see there to come together and collectively love.

Tripping on the Future: Parliament-Funkadelia

Funk + LSD = Funk Psychedelicized = Psychedelia Funkatized = Funkadelia.

Kodwo Eshun, *More Brilliant Than the Sun*

George Clinton — an interstellar musician from a galaxy far, far away — arrived in Detroit from the future. He began as a singer in the barbershop quartet, the Parliaments. Named after the cigarette brand, Clinton's eventual turn to apocalyptic psychedelia implies they were smoking something far more potent. Working for years at scoring the Parliaments a hit, Clinton finally got his foot in the music industry's door when he gained employment as a Motown producer in the late Sixties. Making trips to and from Detroit, he delivered the Parliaments their first hit, "I Wanna Testify." Grabbing the funk formula of James Brown and Sly & the Family Stone, the tune kicked off an acid-washed era for the group. Shortly after the single's release, due to contractual issues, the band would splinter, reconfigure and expand into Funkadelic.

Signing to Detroit's Westbound label, Parliament-Funkadelic would begin to explore LSD. For Clinton, acid was a form of anger management, a way to redirect rage and slip into new ways of perceiving the world. As he said, "I could get mad enough at the world and how it was treating people to wait in an alley and kill some mothafucka." Continuing, Clinton explained, "But there ain't no winning in a situation like that. Once we got out of there, I'd take acid to make sure I didn't get that mad no more. I'd start looking at, you know, alternate realities." These alternate realities would become the conceit of the entire Funkadelic project, aligning the collective with the creative movement Afrofuturism.

Coined by cultural theorist Mark Derry in 1993,

Afrofuturism is a term used to describe the unique futures offered up by black artists. While the future in popular culture is usually looked at through a white lens, the defining feature of Afrofuturist work is its centering of black people as agents in the future. In order to achieve this, Afrofuturism commonly links black struggles from the past to the present and then a future where they've been overcome. Clinton embodies this with his Star Child persona, an extra-terrestrial musician who has just landed a UFO on stage from space, but also the future. This is exemplified by the band's live show at the time, which found the group quite literally landing their mothership on stage each night, decked out in various cosmonaut costumes. Lyrically, we also see this in the track "Mothership Connection" from 1975.

The conceit of Funkadelic's 1970 album *Free Your Mind... and Your Ass Will Follow* was to see if the group could cut a whole record while tripping on acid. Indeed, from its inception, the Parliament-Funkadelic project was based on a black psychedelia that entailed psychic liberation. We might think of Funkadelic as scientists using acid as an accelerant to enlightenment. Clinton and his band turned inward, managing to find salvation in a world that was crushing economic progress and assassinating Civil Rights leaders. Four years following *Free Your Mind*, Clinton would echo a similar sentiment in perhaps the group's most profound track, "Good Thoughts, Bad Thoughts." Culminating in a beautiful poem seemingly delivered from God, Clinton informs us that the path is where you "change your mind," and thus "change your relation to time." In Detroit, time is out of joint, but in a uniquely positive way. Clinton continues, "The kingdom of heaven is within you, free your mind and your ass will follow." When we liberate the mind, the vessel that carries it comes along for the ride.

The collective's trajectory of acid liberation reached

fever-pitch with their next record, 1971's *Maggot Brain* — an album that moves us into the future. Robert Christgau describes the record as "druggy time-warped shlock" with "a rhythm so pronounced and eccentric it could make Berry Gordy twitch to death." Indeed, the record is a sort of death-trip, beginning with Eddie Hazel's ten-minute, funerary guitar solo. As the legend commonly goes, Hazel — dosed on LSD — was advised by Clinton to think of the saddest thing he could, which turned out to be his mother dying. The resulting solo is a direct expression of despair at imagining the ones we love most underground, while maggots crawl in their brain. Anchored by an angelic guitar arpeggio, "Maggot Brain" finds Hazel playing a wah-wah-washed, feedback-drenched solo that takes the work of Hendrix to new heights. In mourning his own mother, and simultaneously Mother Earth, Hazel goes to the mountaintops. Hazel's love and sorrow even takes us higher than Detroit's cloud-penetrating, chrome-plated skyscrapers. If we allow ourselves to get lost in the track's meditative trance, we find ourselves in the expanding vacuum of space, the eternal plane of the sorrowful mind. Once again, lost in the feedback.

According to Emily Lordi, in a *New York Times* piece from 2022, *Maggot Brain*'s opening trip illustrates "the distinction between Black psychedelia and the science fiction-based strain of Black creative pursuit that it would energize (with Clinton at the helm): Afrofuturism." Lordi goes on to write:

> While Afrofuturists such as Sun Ra, Samuel R. Delany and Octavia E. Butler tended to privilege future worlds or outer space — the "absolute otherwhere," as the Black poet Robert Hayden once wrote — Black psychedelics tended to focus on the present, the earthly plane. Lordi's central

argument is that "Black psychedelia was its own artistic movement, and often a feminist one."

This novel distinction is extremely useful, as it helps us situate the Temptations' *Cloud Nine* and *Psychedelic Shack* as well as the Supremes' "Stoned Love." While Sun Ra, Lee "Scratch" Perry and George Clinton were off to the literal cosmos, the black psychedelics of Detroit were taking a trip on *terra firma*, exploring the solar system of the mind. Black psychedelia extends out to and cross-pollinates with acid communism. Recall that acid communism boils down to

> the convergence of class consciousness, socialist-feminist consciousness-raising and psychedelic consciousness, the fusion of new social movements with a communist project, an unprecedented aestheticization of everyday life.

Feminism and psychedelic consciousness go hand-in-hand, something attested to by the centrality of the Supremes to Motown's psychedelic soul. Moreover, Lordi suggests that black psychedelia is powerful because it points to the notion that it's not necessary to leave Earth in order to envision a world radically different from our own. The idea we can extract is that the better world, the post-capitalist future we dream of, can be built right here on our contested planet's fertile soil.

For all their outlandishness compared to, say, the dapper and demure Marvin Gaye, even Parliament-Funkadelic never strayed too far from the political, and indeed, one of their biggest influences was MC5, who embedded the Detroit music scene with a commitment to revolutionary ideas. While Parliament-Funkadelic might have been imagining a world far out beyond our own, in terms of their day-to-day practice we again see the theme of black collectivity back at the forefront. Modeled after Sly

Stone, Clinton may have been the conductor, but — as if they weren't already madly prolific enough — the project would spawn a family tree that included a cast of influential characters. Both Eddie "Maggot Brain" Hazel and bassist William "Bootsy" Collins would produce a series of solo records and side projects. Meanwhile, the group featured Walter "Junie" Morrison from the Ohio Players; prolific session player Jerome "Bigfoot" Bailey, who'd go on to start the band Mutiny; and synthesizer wizard Bennie Worrell. Further, four original members of P-Funk — "Shady Grady" Thomas, Fuzzy Haskins, Ray Davis, Calvin Simon — would go on to form the sprawling side group Original P. There were also two women-led spinoff groups — the Brides of Frankenstein and Parlet. Later, Clinton would link up with influential musician Amp Fiddler, who played with Enchantment, mentored J Dilla, and went on to become a staple in Detroit's electronic music scene. Clinton, who was inspired by Frank Zappa, no doubt created something of his own surrogate family freak scene. Ultimately, his dedication to cultivating a collective spirit remained a part of Detroit, and we'll see it re-emerge in all the subsequent scenes we explore.

4. ELECTRIC ENTOURAGE: DETROIT MEETS DUSSELDORF

The mentality of the machines, considering the assembly lines of the automotive companies, we've gotten our inspiration from that decay.
                    Carl Craig, *Techno City: What is Detroit Techno?*

In the late 1970s, in the Metro Detroit suburb of Belleville, Michigan, a trio of young music-makers would reconfigure the past decade of Detroit sounds into a new strain — the next evolution — of Afrofuturism and black psychedelic music. Influenced in equal parts by robotic German krautrock, Motown's machine funk, synth-heavy new wave, and house records coming out of Chicago, techno emerged as a unique musical phenomenon that — like all of the music we've discussed so far — could have only taken root in the Motor City. In this chapter, we'll trace the history of Detroit techno and investigate the underlying philosophy of this genre that would give its birthplace the nickname "Techno City."

The story of techno begins at Belleville High School, with an unlikely alliance between three high school students who shared a love for burgeoning new technologies, science fiction, chess, and an eclectic array of music. Juan Atkins, Kevin Saunderson, and Derrick May — the Originator, the Elevator, and the Innovator respectively — would come to be known as the Belleville Three, but for now they were just high school kids playing sports while imbibing heady ideas about the future and a diverse swath of records.

Juan Atkins had first been exposed to a synthesizer at a young age, and it became one of his instruments of choice. In Detroit music history, the synthesizer takes us back to the sci-fi sounding introduction of the Supremes' "Reflections," Stevie Wonder's early Seventies records like *Talking Book* and *Innervisions* and Funkadelic's 1978 party-starter "Flashlight." On his tenth birthday, Atkins received a guitar from his father. By his teen years, precocious Juan was playing in garage-funk bands that could be heard all throughout his neighborhood. Providing the link to his musical comrades was Juan's younger brother, Aaron, who played football with Derrick May and Kevin Saunderson. Upon befriending them, the teenaged Juan passed Derrick a mixtape containing tracks from Tangerine Dream and Giorgio Moroder. Between the time spent at football practices, the new friends would continue to bond over records. Living just a stone's throw from the Detroit airport, we can imagine them looking up to the skies, seeing planes taking people to faraway lands, dreaming of decadent European discotheques. As it would turn out, visions of glitzy European — specifically Berliner — nightlife would inspire the trio from across the Atlantic.

The Electrifyin' Mojo and the German Connection

Supplying the tunes that satisfied the trio's voracious musical appetite was the essential DJ Charles Johnson, better known as the Electrifyin' Mojo. Johnson was a Vietnam veteran who got his start as a DJ for his fellow troops, an experience that gave him first-hand knowledge of all genres of music. After the war, Johnson's wide-ranging music appreciation would return with him to Detroit. In the 2006 film *The Cycles of the Mental Machine*, on Mojo and the legacy of Detroit, he says, "I always wanted to be just a face in the background: a voice on the radio, a face in a crowd, a figment of the imagination. I've always believed music has tremendous power." Indeed, Johnson built his brand around facelessness and anonymity, something that remains part of techno's ethos to this day.

According to Juan Atkins in Michaelangelo Matos's epic chronicle of rave *The Underground is Massive*, "Mojo was one of the first FM DJ icons," and his show *The Midnight Funk Association* was "the first black station that had an AOR format — they would play the whole side of an album." Taking a page out of fellow Detroiter George Clinton's playbook, each night Mojo would land his Mothership on-air for his avid, widespread Detroit listenership. Mojo would begin by asking the members of the Midnight Funk Association to rise, and like allegiant troops, they did. He would then instruct his loyal devotees to switch on and off their porch lights or flash their car lights in an act of solidarity, which they also did. In our age where mass communication has been sapped of community and creativity, it's easy to see from the very beginning how Mojo captured the hearts and minds of those within his bandwidth.

It was Mojo's decidedly futurist approach and assorted selection of Parliament-Funkadelic, James Brown and the B-52s that simultaneously broke down the city's racialized music barriers and inspired techno. Indeed, there's no overstating Mojo's profound influence on the shaping of the city's love of music from all across the stylistic spectrum. As a testament to his taste-making, take an example from 2021, when I attended a DJ set from Detroit house legend Moodymann on the riverfront at the Aretha Franklin Amphitheater. On a humid and rainy summer night, the veteran producer opened his set saying, "I can't help myself, I still love this stuff," and proceeded to play a death-disco mix of the B-52s's surf-rock track "Planet Claire." Only a

Detroit DJ who grew up on the influence of Mojo would find it fit to play such a track, and only in Detroit would it land so well with the crowd. More than taste-making, some believe Mojo's on-air presence even contributed to the end of gang warfare in Detroit. According to "Mad" Mike Banks, "that Summer gang warfare was at a height and Mojo would get on the radio and ask for peace, pray for peace, and then drop the B-52s, man."

Around this same time, another DJ known as the Wizard was making waves on-air and at parties. His name was Jeff Mills, and he would go on to become a Detroit techno legend. His star was so solidified that, in some circles, asking for "Jeff Mills" became slang for requesting pills. For now though, Mills was an emerging titan known for spinning electro, Chicago house, and industrial records. As it stands, thanks to Mojo and the Wizard, surf-rock riffs sound just at home in a Detroit DJ set as hard-hitting house beats. But the group that would prove most instrumental in the formation of both electro and techno weren't Americans at all, but rather a band of German robots.

Kraftwerk's influence on techno is so significant and far-reaching that many even argue that they're the inventors of the genre, and that, if not in Detroit, techno originated in their hometown of Dusseldorf, Germany. What we see here is the continuation of a dynamic interplay between Detroit and Germany that stems all the way back to the Stooges' embrace of avant-garde composers. With the Stooges in mind, we ought not to forget that Iggy was lingering in Berlin at this very moment with Bowie and Brian Eno, making records that would earn them Kraftwerk's respect. Detroit and Germany's symbiotic relationship, in which they would continually respond to each other's musical developments, was reinforced by similarly constricting socio-political circumstances. The circulation of influence can quickly be summarized as follows: avant-garde German composers like Stockhausen influenced Detroit proto-punk rockers the Stooges; the Stooges and the punk movement in Detroit were inspiration to German krautrock groups like Can, Neu!, and Kraftwerk; Kraftwerk inspired the Belleville Three; Detroit techno goes on to become a staple of German club culture. Additionally, Motown's black psychedelia from Diana Ross & the Supremes would merge with Kraftwerk's synthesizer work in the form of time-bending disco tunes like "I'm Coming Out" and Donna Summer's "I Feel Love."

Both Detroit, home of the motor industry, and Germany share a similarly haunted preoccupation with automobiles. Volkswagen was a state-owned company founded by Hitler himself which broke ground when the Autobahn began construction, and a line runs through from the automobile worship that can be found on Kraftwerk's breakthrough single, 1974's "Autobahn," a twenty-two-minute ode to driving on the iconic German freeway, into techno, where we see the idea of cruising into the Afrofuturist epoch to come in Cybotron's trailblazing 1982 track "Cosmic Cars." Equally, we could look at Carl Craig's techno ode to late-night driving in Detroit, "Red Lights." But more than this, techno reproduces the *feel* of frictionless high-speed cruising through a vectoral city of the mind, out of the Age of Affluence and into the Leisure Age. If the motorik drum patterns from Krautrock bands like Neu! are filled with a sense of propulsion and forward momentum, and if you can still hear the pistons and valves pumping in Kraftwerk's rickety rhythms, then techno has us accelerating into the ice-cool future in a souped-up Delorean, the car designed by disgraced Detroit visionary John DeLorean, the emblem of the future used by Marty and Doc to travel through time in the *Back to the Future* films.

Kraftwerk not only pioneered techno's sound with their implementation of icy synthesizer arpeggios and programmed drum beats, but its aesthetic and philosophy too. Indeed, it was not their music alone that merely suggested the machinic, they themselves performed as automatons. If Gordy had composed songs to the rhythm of the machines, Kraftwerk seemed to be the machines themselves. The quintet wore identical white-collar clothes on stage and performed in jerky movements that imitated B-movie androids. Nowhere is their carbon-copy aesthetic clearer than on the sleeve of their landmark 1978 LP, *The Man Machine*. Streaked with a modernist red-and-black title graphic and the quintet appearing as plastic mannequins, we find the first traces of techno's posthuman flair. The fact that Kraftwerk were first and foremost robots assembled from circuits and switchboards, not Germans of flesh and bone, struck a chord with Detroit techno musicians.

What is Techno?

Techno properly started with the Belleville Three, those three young men who shared a love for Mojo's music in their high school years. If one of them can be said to be the godfather, it is Juan Atkins, also known as "the one" and "the originator." Since high school, Atkins considered himself a serious artist and, shortly after graduation, formed his first real project, the electro duo Cybotron with Vietnam War veteran Rick Davis. The group's 1983 debut record, *Enter*, contains the blueprint for techno: four-on-the-floor beats, stabbing synthesizer lines, bouncing bass, and pitched robotic vocals.

Simultaneously, Atkins was DJing regularly with a party crew featuring Derrick May and newcomer Eddie Fowlkes. Working their way up the echelons of Detroit's elite party scene, the DJ crew, known as Deep Space Soundworks, began to establish a reputation for themselves. Earning massive respect around town, the Deep Space crew would even link up with their inspiration — Mojo — who championed Juan as a prodigy and granted the clique radio airtime for under-the-table mixing.

The following five years — 1983 through 1987 — would prove to be a gestation period, with the Belleville Three, Eddie Fowlkes, and others developing and riffing off the techno template established by Cybotron. The Belleville Three and other DJs would begin to credit their records to various monikers: Juan Atkins going by Model 500 and Infiniti; Derrick May as Mayday and Rhythim is Rhythim; and Kevin Saunderson as Tronik House, Reese, Essaray and E-Dancer. As Mark Fisher wrote, the move was fitting "for a sound that was so depersonalized and dehumanized, with names of the acts tending to be cryptic cyberpunk tags, disconnected from any biography or place." In this fertile few years, notable singles include Model 500's "No UFOs," Technicolor's "Channel One," X-Ray's "Let's Go," and most important of all, Derrick May's timeless "Strings of Life."

"Strings of Life," with its stuttering synthesizer and abnormally joyful piano, proved to be a crossover hit in the Chicago house scene, further establishing a strong alliance with Windy City titans Frankie Knuckles and Farley "Jackmaster" Funk. While house was melodious, more in-line with disco, and decidedly queer, techno is cold, rhythmic and — on its surface — devoid of any libidinal appeals. Derrick May's 1987 single brilliantly fuses the best of both of these worlds.

It's easy to imagine techno as an underground phenomenon that only the culturally tapped-in, well-informed few might have been aware of. However, this was anything but the case. Techno was ubiquitous in Detroit in the 1980s, evidenced by Mojo and Ken "The Godfather of House" Collier championing it on the airwaves. It was spun all over town by DJ crews at parties. However, the Detroit party scene quickly began to reflect class divisions within the black community, as party promoters took great pains to make sure that only middle and upper-class patrons were admitted, echoing the emphasis on exclusivity in European fashion culture, which techno was heavily inspired by. These teen parties included Charivari, which would inspire and spin A Number of Names' pioneering techno anthem "Sharevari", where the glossy jet-setting European lifestyle was a major influence, with ravers taking fashion cues from magazines that touted high-society lifestyles like *GQ*, *Vogue*, *Interview* and more. For the musicians, when the scene got caught up in exclusion is precisely when it lost its power.

Further solidifying techno's place in the local mainstream was Detroit's *The New Dance Show*, a sort of cyborg soul train hosted by R.J. Watkins, which featured a crew of beloved regular dancers. Spinning off from the long-running Detroit dance show *The Scene*, *The New Dance Show* took on a distinctly techno-oriented approach, highlighting several of the city's key players on-air. One of the greatest, most joyous moments of *The New Dance Show*'s programming features the regular participants doing a dance-line to the promethean 1987 Detroit anthem "Good Life" by Inner City, a Kevin Saunderson project featuring immortal vocal parts from Paris Grey. As of 2022, this iconic moment of Detroit history is documented on YouTube for your digital time-traveling pleasures.

Industrial Lies

Techno arrived at a unique point in the city's history, as Diego Rivera's proletarian dream of Detroit was being thwarted by neoliberal privatization, crushed workers' movements, corporate abandonment, and a continuing exodus of the upper-middle class to the growing suburbs. This beginning-of-the-end moment in Detroit history is rendered most succinctly in Paul Schrader's "accidently

Marxist" 1978 film *Blue Collar*, which depicts that same site of Rivera's mural — the factory — now as a contested zone of safety and solidarity.

With one of the greatest directorial debuts in cinematic history, Schrader — hot off the heels of screenwriting Scorsese's *Taxi Driver* — arrived with a film that follows three Ford auto factory workers — Zeke, Jerry, and Smokey — played by the tour de force trifecta of Richard Pryor, Harvey Keitel, and Yapphet Kotto respectively. The opening series of shots of workers along the factory line synced-up to Captain Beefheart's blues romp "Hard Working Man" sets the stage. With percussion that clangs like heavy machinery, you'd be forgiven for thinking the song was using sounds from the factory itself. This opening sequence delivers an image of a truly mechanical, auto factory blues.

Playing with the traditions of genre, Schrader uses the heist film as a way of revealing the socio-economic reality of Detroit at this time: increasingly unaffordable bills, indebtedness, and worsening conditions. The solution for the protagonists is to resort to robbing the corrupt and racist union's office. But — by giving us glimpses into Zeke and Jerry's family life — *Blue Collar* makes it explicitly clear that these are characters whose criminal motives come from a deeply human place of love and necessity. Never for a moment does the film forget to remind you of the harsh reality of borderline poverty's constant pressure: debts never seem to stop piling up, leisure time slowly slips away, paranoia and pressure builds. The characters are always just shy of meeting their families' basic needs.

When the corporation teams up with the FBI to identify our heroes as the guilty parties, the lines of solidarity amongst the trio are truly tested for the first time. To escape trouble, Zeke accepts a promotion, moving up echelons of the corrupt union. Meanwhile, Jerry's family is threatened and he is pressured to sell-out to the feds. Tragically, it's the hardened badass of the group, Smokey — the one most prepared to challenge the system — that is killed in a calculated "workplace accident." All of the pressure and paranoia proves to be too much, and ultimately the film builds up an explosive confrontation between Zeke — now a foreman — and an FBI-protected Jerry hurling racist epithets at each other on the factory floor. They charge at each other, and right as they're about to strike, the film stops on a freeze-frame, forcing us to linger on how these former friends who bowled with each other's families have been broken by the corporate system. Like a prophetic martyr, one of Smokey's famous lines — a sage critique of neoliberal capitalism from an earlier confessional in the film — is echoed over the chilling final tableaux: "They pit the lifers against the new boy and the young against the old. The black against the white. Everything they do is to keep us in our place."

If *Blue Collar* depicts the late 1970s as the beginning of the end for Detroit's boom period, then by the 1980s, with the city's implosion accelerating, Motor City had evolved into something resembling what Mark Fisher called "the eerie." According to Fisher, the eerie is a place where "there is nothing present when there should be something," which for Fisher commonly means "landscapes partially emptied of the human." And by the 1980s, Detroit was increasingly filled with dead zones of abandoned neighborhoods, derelict warehouses, vast abandoned factories and overgrown fields, all bearing the traces of their former inhabitants. Detroit journalist Charlie LeDuff dubbed these grassy overgrowths where the land has reclaimed its territory "ghost gardens". *Nothing where there should be something.* Driving through Detroit in the 1980s might have prompted questions such as: "What happened to produce these ruins, this disappearance? What kind of entity was involved? What kind of thing was it that emitted such an eerie cry?"

Specters of Detroit

Ah, no nostalgia hurts as much as nostalgia for things that never existed!

Fernando Pessoa, *The Book of Disquiet*

In the 2000s, Mark Fisher used the term "hauntology" to describe a moment in which artists were confronting a cultural impasse. The term was borrowed from the 1994 book *Spectres of Marx* by deconstructionist philosopher Jacques Derrida, who wrote on the way the ideas of Karl Marx had persisted despite the then-recent fall of the Soviet Union and the "end of history" narrative being trumpeted by Francis Fukuyama. To describe this phenomenon, Derrida coined the neologism "hauntology", a pun on the words "haunt" and "ontology." If ontology is the study of being, it follows that hauntology is the study of a hauntedness, simultaneous presence and absence.

This central concept was initially explored in a somewhat different register by Fisher's friend and sparring partner Simon Reynolds in his 2010 book *Retromania*. According to Reynolds, the 2000s were the "re" decade, a moment characterized by revivals, reissues, and reunions. Fisher and Reynolds were arguing that the weight of referencing and self-consciousness in postmodern art had caved in on itself, producing a dead end where the new no longer seemed possible. Moreover, they declaratively wrote that cultural time had flattened due to the widespread inability to do anything but look back to the past. Hauntological music, argued Fisher, was the cultural response to this moment out of time.

Importantly, according to Fisher, hauntological musicians like the Caretaker and Burial do not merely reproduce and refurbish sounds of the past — rather, they consciously critique a moment of stasis by acknowledging the deadlock brought on by the grip of the past. While Fisher had a deep and abiding interest in techno, he never looked at it through the lens of hauntology, perhaps because of its avowed and audible sonic radicalism. Yet it's Detroit techno, I'd suggest, that provides us in some ways with an early example of a music form that confronts the ghosts of the past, and in doing so overcomes them.

With regard to Kraftwerk, one of techno's formative influences, the American poet and critic Cynthia Cruz notes in her book *The Melancholia of Class* that, "When you listen to Kraftwerk [...], there is a dark undercurrent within which one feels a sense of haunting, where the past seems to enter." It is obvious what legacy the German youth of the Sixties and Seventies may have been haunted by and running away from. The crystalline, deep space motorik of Neu!'s grooves powering the mothership on through the nebula, or Kraftwerk's odes to a depersonalized but deeply poignant aesthetic of the neon lights, sky labs, and personal computers, point toward a pristine computer world full of sedated, passionless subjects unstained by blood or soil. But century-long dreams and devastating losses are equally hardwired into techno's DNA, music from a city the majority of whose black residents had traveled to from the South, only to be hit within short order by the increasingly devastating waves of unemployment about to sweep through the city. These are also phantoms of Detroit's utopian promises: the promised workers' benefits of Fordism, the decriminalization of marijuana advocated by John Sinclair and the White Panthers, neighborhoods organizing self-sustaining communal networks, and the cultural ambassadorship of Motown. These were the futures that tuckered out, that were dying before many of the city's inhabitants had even begun to participate in them.

Detroit techno therefore also carries some of the ambiguity that Cruz's sensitive ear detects in Kraftwerk. Techno is ostensibly a celebratory vision of man merging with machine, new regimes of dispassionate delights, Old European poise. It was a forecast of these machine-tooled comforts that Motor City techno built its worldwide reputation on, from the start both clinging to that vision of a promised land and equally being unable to escape the reality of what is happening all around it. As Cybotron sings on track three of their seminal record *Clear*, it seems that the corporation's promises of a better future for Detroit were "just industrial lies," in which capitalist powers only cared for three things: "maximize, profitize, exploitation." This foreboding vision of what was to come is spelled out further in the title of Detroit In Effect's single "There Ain't No Future." Take as a further example Juan Atkins' track under the moniker Model 500, "No UFOs." Considered the first ever techno single, "No UFOs" seems to comment on the failure of the future. In the glory days of technological progress, it seemed plausible to believe that flying cars, jet packs, and commercial space shuttles were just around the corner. However, as Atkins understood, there would be no UFOs hovering over Detroit anytime soon.

For many techno musicians, memories of the future involved man and machine coexisting at maximum efficiency in a utopian dream city, as world-historically significant, monumental, and chic as Paris or Berlin. In the wake of the post-Fordist fallout, lost futures were hardwired into the sonic structure of techno with producers taking inspiration from decaying machinery in the city's automobile factories. The Belleville Three's synthesizer pad sequences are chillingly cold, and their programmed drums are equally devoid of the distinctly human bounce. Yet, this process of reacting against and refracting Motown is precisely what haunts the records of Reese and Santonio, Eddie Fowlkes, Carl Craig and more. Ultimately, these responses to Detroit's past begin to point us in a new direction.

The Second Wave

The first wave of Detroit techno was dominated by the Belleville Three and the network of projects the trio engendered. However, with a new decade on the horizon and the techno sound established, a new crop of Detroit artists were ready to build upon the work of the genre's forefathers. If the first wave had had a schizophrenic approach to their changing social milieu, immersed in its receding promise, haunted by the past and trying to power their way into a Euro-American future that was crumbling around them, then the genre's second wave in the 1990s was characterized by heavier-hitting beats, overt jazz influences, and themes of political militancy, which directly fought against the city's weakening infrastructure and big industry co-optation.

In 1989, Jeff Mills, "Mad" Mike Banks, and Robert "Noise" Hood (AKA the Vision) would form Underground Resistance, a militant techno collective dedicated to infusing their minimalist beats with themes of social activism. Central to Underground Resistance's mission was steering young black men away from drug gangs. Like most techno labels, Underground Resistance were strictly dedicated to a DIY approach that allowed them to circumvent the clutches of the music industry while simultaneously going on to achieve international success. Amongst the most outspokenly political collectives to emerge out of Detroit, the group firmly linked techno to a progressive ideology that championed autonomy and anti-capitalism. Like their hip-hop contemporaries Public Enemy, Underground Resistance — often performing in ski masks — would imbue techno with a new consciousness-raising ethos on tracks like "Message to the Majors" and "Transition."

The importance of Underground Resistance was not lost on Fisher, who miraculously secured a rare interview opportunity with Mike Banks for British magazine the *Wire* in 2007. He opens the piece, entitled "Agents of Disorder," by setting the scene, providing the context that, "Since 1989, Detroit techno collective Underground Resistance have been locked in a struggle against the global forces of Capital corroding the social fabric of their city," and describes Banks himself as an "engineer of collectivity, sonic and political theorist and techgnostic televisionary." What follows is one of the most brilliant exchanges in music journalism history.

Remarking on the location of the interview, the Hague, Fisher echoes the sentiment that, "Detroit Techno has always been about a strange transit between Europe and the USA." Banks begins the interview stating that, like the shifting automotive industry, Detroit techno musicians now "face competition from all over the world. So, what used to be your territory only, now is shared by many." Later in the article, Fisher, clamping down on the way in which Underground Resistance understood that the medium *is* the message, notes that "Banks made an anti-egoistic ethic out of techno's anonymity, refusing to be photographed or to play the PR game according to the media's personalizing rules." Out of this, Banks agrees that the commitment to never surfacing is part of their appeal:

> I think that's what people enjoy about UR, they get to paint their own picture. We might just make the canvas for them with the record... We just went faceless. There was no reason

for you to know what we look like, you just concentrate more on what the sound was.

An interesting juncture comes when Banks and Fisher find common ground in the way that making art can possess a person, the body becoming a vessel that's making way for a bigger spirit to move through. Banks discusses this in relation to his soulful, hi-tech jazz recordings, while Fisher maintains he's felt something similar when writing blogposts.

Despite coming from seemingly disparate worlds, Fisher and Banks come off as kindred spirits with lots in common. Perhaps part of the reason they hit it off so quickly is because they're both what Robert Hood called "spectral nomads," "those adept at moving clandestinely between the mesh of Capital's worldwide web." Perhaps the most prescient insight Fisher makes is that

the UR collective offer some kind of future for a Detroit youth that would otherwise be denied one. If Motown was the pop parallel to Fordist car production, UR are the Techno antidote to some of the ravages of post-Fordist capital.

This is because — crucially — Underground Resistance stayed in Detroit, acting, like so many other techno musicians, as mentors, talent scouts, and champions of the city's local scenes. Further, Banks talks about his — sometimes discouraging — experience as a Detroit high school baseball coach. Ultimately, it's all part of a resistance, an "electronic warfare aimed at deprogramming a population addicted and stupefied by late capitalism's stimulus blitz." If it's a battle, then it's not one of in-fighting, of black versus white, but rather "a war between programmers and fugitives, between overground normality and underground gnosis, between a history given over to atrocity and exploitation and an empty future waiting to be populated."

Like the Parliament-Funkadelic nexus before them, Underground Resistance spawned a sprawling network of notable techno musicians and projects. These include, but are not limited to, Suburban Knight, DJ Rolando, Punisher, Galaxy 2 Galaxy — purveyors of a musical style called Hi Tech Jazz — and the great Drexciya, a techno duo composed of James Stinson and Gerald Donald of Dopplereffekt.

Drexciya were discovered by Mike Banks, who called them "some of the weirdest space shit I ever heard." They are built upon a foundation of Afrofuturist lore, with the duo's name coming from the Afrofuturist story of Drexciya, an underwater country said to be home to descendants of the African women thrown overboard from slave ships. The duo is committed to defamiliarizing sonic templates, opening up techno to another blue world of languid beats and ambient meditations. If techno is to some degree haunted by the past, Drexciya are a perfect example of a hauntological approach — their tracks, intent on evoking images of a strange new Earth, are also the sonic analogues of a story about taking collective trauma and remorselessly creating a new mythos, which invites in ghosts but banishes energy-sapping specters. Performing in masks, Drexciya follow in the footsteps of their Underground Resistance label by cleaving to an anonymity that they maintained throughout their career. By the time they had released only their first five EPs, Drexciya were being hailed as part of a vanguard of freaky new Detroit techno. Right on the precipice of what was thought to be the Y2K meltdown, Drexciya released their classic 1999 LP *Neptune's Lair*, followed by 2002's beloved *Harnessed The Storm*.

Rising to the forefront of the second wave of Detroit

techno was a DJ named Carl Craig. A direct descendent of the Belleville Three, Craig would release his spectral masterpiece, *More Songs About Food and Revolutionary Art*, in 1997. Riffing off of the title of Talking Heads second record, the LP again showcases the ways in which, just by packaging records with anonymous white labels or politically charged titles, it was possible to lay out the trajectory of an entire sonic fiction for listeners to project onto often lyricless songs. Featuring tracks like the ghostly "Red Lights," the album perfectly captures the feeling of a night drive through Detroit's desolate streets. Rather than zooming through space in a cosmic car, Craig and other second-wave techno musicians ground their records in the Earthly realm where truth is stranger than science fiction. On this Earth, capital dominates the psyche and compromises culture. This is a vision in which the posthuman subject is cross-hatched with fiber optics, augmented and enmeshed, driven through the ruined night by desires that are not their own.

If Rivera's mural captured Detroit's Fordist era, and Schrader's *Blue Collar* did the same for its decline into post-Fordism, then it is Paul Verhoeven's 1987 film *RoboCop* that best captures this third, cybernetic era of Detroit history. In *RoboCop*'s future vision of Detroit, humans are augmented not for their own gain, but capital's. RoboCop, a resurrected first responder, stalks the dystopian streets of burned-out "Old Detroit" for the purposes of the eradication of crime. Once his mission is complete, corporations can begin building "Delta City," a sleek new home of the hivemind. RoboCop the character is haunted by submerged memories of his former human self, whereas *RoboCop* the film is preoccupied with the memories of a future Detroit. The film is rightly revered as a great, parodic vision of the despoiled future we were cruising into in 1987, asleep at the wheel. Yet, if the film fails on any front, it's the score.

The classical orchestral soundtrack is all wrong, and we can much more easily imagine sequences of cyberpunk Detroit overlaid with the chilling techno of the Belleville clique, evoking both the future and a dark vision of the past.

Today, techno persists in Detroit, with many second-wave musicians still DJing their favorite local haunts. Meanwhile, first-wave legends stake a claim for their legacy and legend when they headline the city's towering Movement Festival, the USA's premiere electronic music fest. In 2022, I was able to catch Juan Atkins and Kevin Saunderson as E-Dancer, following each other for headlining sets. Other highlights of the weekend included the acid king Richie Hawtin, a staple of the fest since it began in 2000; Jeff Mills; and Detroit third-wave pioneer DJ Stingray 313. For the past two decades, the festival, located right in downtown's Hart Plaza, has been a crucial event, bringing in electronica fans from across the world. It serves as a powerful reminder of how electronic dance music — which has travelled far and wide since the 1980s — began right here in this city of lost and found futures.

In *Acid Communism*, Fisher reminds us that, "The past has to be continually re-narrated, and the political point of reactionary narratives is to suppress the potentials which still await, ready to be re-awakened, in older moments." What suppressed potentials still await, ready to be re-awakened, within techno? As we have seen, techno — a fundamentally futurist music form — was in large part stalked by the ghosts of Detroit's turbulent history, but still managed to break free from them. Techno musicians responded to the oppressive weight of history not with pastiche or stasis, but a decidedly modernist move towards the new. They were cunning in their ability to circumvent any exploitative engagement with the music industry and paved a way for themselves that kept their communities involved in the music-making process. If the story of

Detroit techno matters today, it is for these reasons. In our own troubled cultural times of reunions, revivals, and reissues, we can remember the story of techno as a source of inspiration for building new musical, cultural, and political futures.

While Detroit's strain of black psychedelic music had brilliantly reconfigured itself in a new, immensely successful strain of dance music, Motor City garage rockers were overcoming their own moment of cultural stasis and socio-economic impasse. Like the techno producers who forged a new way forward, they too would accelerate out of the past with musical innovations that reflected the bleakness of the times. In the next chapter, we will follow the career of one musician in particular, who has weathered the storms of Detroit's turbulent post-Fordist decades.

5. HARDCORE TIMES: THE WASTE LAND OF THE 1980S, OR THE BALLAD OF JOHN BRANNON

Hit top speed, I feel so good, I feel so alive...
Kiss, "Detroit Rock City"

The car crash differs from other disasters in that it involves the most powerfully advertised commercial product of this century, an iconic entity that combines the elements of speed, power, dream and freedom within a highly stylized format that defuses any fears we may have of the inherent dangers of these violent and unstable machines.
J.G. Ballard, The Atrocity Exhibition

The early 1970s saw the last gasps of Detroit's fiery protopunk titans. By 1971, MC5 were on the verge of their implosion, releasing the unheralded *High Time*, a swan song that left fans waiting for more. Meanwhile, the Stooges had dissolved in 1970 after a gig where tensions boiled over at the Goose Lake Festival, Michigan's equivalent to Woodstock. In 1973, Pop reassembled the group as Iggy & the Stooges, releasing that year's incendiary *Raw Power*, an album which contains classic cuts "Search and Destroy" and "Gimme Danger," before the band disintegrated once again. By the late Seventies, things had seemingly moved on all together — Pop was in Berlin with Bowie making art-rock records and the best-selling Detroit artist was back-to-roots rocker Bob Seger.

While the epochal techno scene that was chronicled in

the previous chapter reigned, Detroit rockers returned to the garage to tinker with and recharge their sound. What emerged was different from the music that preceded it, but still a product of the city itself. This new rock sound was born not just from the social and economic hard times that the city found itself in, but also from the spatial and historic dimensions of Detroit's built environment. If the techno innovators drew on the high-tech car and it's cruise mode feature as a model for their sound and style, the rockers mined a different legacy: that of a more recent, confrontational, DIY and underground tradition exemplified by cult car-films of the 1970s like *Vanishing Point* and Monte Hellman's arty and existentialist *Two Lane Blacktop*. In the latter, the protagonists, referred to only as The Driver (James Taylor) and The Mechanic (the Beach Boys' Dennis Wilson) are seekers on a quasi-religious quest for speed. Hellman himself confessed that, "I always thought the film was about speed." They achieve a kind of culmination of this in the film's closing moments, reaching a white-hot pitch of acceleration so intense it burns through the film itself, while the thundering engine and vibrating cab they ride in catches fire, melting away into a pristine beyond.

One key element of *Two Lane Blacktop*'s narrative is the competition between Warren Oates' smooth, older Pontiac (both the name of the character and the car he drives) and the younger, post-hippy Driver and Mechanic in their souped-up Chevrolet. These opposing cars symbolize a generational clash. Representative of the mindsets and social worlds of two epochs — the high-status, high-consumption, comfortable domain of the post-war world and the restless, alienated generation heading into the world's decline — customizing and adapting what remains in the face of an uncertain future (a strategy we'll see more of in the next chapter on the Nineties wave of Detroit rock and hip-hop maestro J Dilla).

In common with the protagonists of *Two Lane Blacktop*, the Motor City has always had an understandable preoccupation with the car, speed, and acceleration — and the hardcore punk scene that emerged in tandem with the social shifts of the 1970s and Eighties pushed musical speed to its limits. The subgenre's roots are easily identifiable with landmark releases like Black Flag's *Nervous Breakdown*, Middle Class's *Out of Vogue*, Dead Kennedys' "California Über Alles" and "Holiday in Cambodia/Police Truck", Germs' *GI*, and Bad Brains' "Pay to Cum!/Stay Close to Me". Yet, no scene pushed hardcore's high-velocity tempo more than the youth crew kids of Detroit in the early 1980s. Though the Detroit hardcore scene of the time encompasses much more, this section will focus on the career of one of those crew kids: John Brannon.

Endowed with one of the most brutal voices in music history, there is no better representative of disaffected Reagan youth than Brannon. Moreover, his several bands reflect the ebbs and flows of Detroit's rock scene between the late 1970s and early 2000s. But before we move on to look at Brannon's life and work, we should jump back slightly to look at the musical and social landscape the hardcore kids were reacting against, which we might be able to sum up in two words: *Bob Seger*.

From Hardhats to Hardcore

Rather than a push into new sonic territory, Bob Seger represented a reinvigorating revamp of the sounds of rock's golden years. Marketing his music as "the real thing," and offering a comfortable sense of the authentically blue collar at a time when older certainties were crashing down all around, Seger dominated the airwaves. He appealed to just about everyone, but much of the appeal was to an anti-disco, working-class, AOR-consuming demographic. As the lyrics of his smash hit "Old Time Rock 'N Roll" have it:

Don't try to take me to a disco
You won't even get me out on the floor
Ten minutes and I'll be late for the door
I love that old time rock 'n roll

In his book *Staying Alive: The Last Days of the Working Class*, Jefferson Cowie notes that the 1970s marked a moment where hardhats and hippies — both of whom could have united in their demands for better working conditions — diverged. This was perhaps most concretely manifested just four hours southwest of Detroit in Chicago at the 1979 Comiskey Park Disco Demolition.

Prompted by the success of disco via *Saturday Night Fever*, disco was at the center of mainstream culture. Proving especially popular in black and queer spaces, disco's liberatory ethos allowed for solidarity on the dance floor. The 12" single allowed records to stretch on, allowing dancers to express themselves and luxuriate in their bodies. Never ones to allow people to enjoy things, masculine rockers responded with the "Disco Sucks" movement. The culmination of this was the Disco Demolition Night — a Major League Baseball promotion centered around blowing up a crate of disco records. When fifty thousand people turned up at Comiskey Park for a double-header faceoff between Detroit's Tigers and Chicago's White Sox, trouble ensued as fans stormed the field, not leaving until riot police ushered them out. As music scholars have rightly pointed out, the event is often read as a collective expression of racism and homophobia. But this pitting of rock against disco is more than just the splintering of hardhats and hippies. Arguably, what we also see in "Disco

Sucks" is the manifestation of tension between a 1950s-oriented, backward-looking white culture in conflict with a technophile, future-directed generation creating primarily black culture, composed and supportive of any number of minority cultures and identities. In a sense, "Disco Sucks" is in many respects a first manifestation of what we now routinely refer to as "the Culture War."

Politics aside, Seger's polished, rust-belt rock 'n roll is still championed by music fans from across the political spectrum in Michigan. His raspy voice and perfectly calculated chord changes are ideal for driving down desolate Midwest highways, and we ought to note in passing the undeniable triumph that was his late-Seventies trifecta of records: 1976's *Night Moves*, 1978's *Stranger in Town*, and 1980's *Against the Wind*. By 1981, animation legend Ralph Bakshi found it fitting to cast Seger's music as the embodiment of American music in his own opus, the film *American Pop*.

The thesis that Detroit was some sort of rock 'n roll haven in the late 1970s was further advanced by power-pop rockers Kiss on their 1976 single "Detroit Rock City," which was actually inspired by a fan dying on the way to a gig. According to Paul Stanley, they were "thinking how weird it is that people's lives end so quickly. People can be on their way to something that's really a party and a celebration of being alive and die in the process of doing it." To be fair to Kiss, if they were thinking of the confluence of artists that included the highly polished professionalism of the likes of Bob Seger, Mitch Ryder & the Detroit Wheels, and Ted Nugent, then, well, they had a point: Detroit *rocked*.

Night Moves, Necros and Need for a Scene

Seger and his Detroit peers had put the city's music scene into a slick but profitable holding pattern by the late

Seventies, and for many in Detroit, there was a growing restlessness and need for some new blood. Disaffected youth were searching for an attitude and an aesthetic that could look, if not to the future, then at least at the increasingly crumbling present and vent their frustration. Arriving from Ohio, delinquent punks Necros expressed just that, with an approach that was a complete distillation of adolescent snottiness and refusal. The band's 1979 *Ambionic Sound* is complete with teenage rippers such as "I Hate My School," "Peer Pressure," and "Public School." Nestled among these adolescent ragers are two politically tinted cuts that despair at how little progress had been made since the Civil Rights movement: "Police Brutality" and "Race Riot." The former would turn out to be a staple recording for the band, appearing on the 1981 *Sex Drive* 7" and 1983 LP *Conquest for Death*. Though they are seldom given credit, the group's speedy playing and raw rage on these early releases are among the founding documents of hardcore punk. Around this same time, the teenage Necros befriended scene legend Tesco Vee, founder of influential hardcore bastion Touch and Go Records and front man of Detroit band the Meatmen. At the same time, John Brannon entered the fray, whose career we will trace in the rest of this section.

We will approach Brannon's prolific career and series of stylistic and sonic iterations through Elizabeth Kubler-Ross's "five stages of grief." First formulated in her landmark 1969 book, *On Death and Dying*, Kubler-Ross offers up a powerful analysis of mourning and facing our inescapable fates, and outlines the five stages of grief that people go through when grappling with their impending death or the passing of a loved one. These five stages are: denial, anger, bargaining, depression, and acceptance. Trying to exactly separate out the different strands of loss is of course fruitless and, as I'll argue, Brannon's musical arc plays out like a lifelong struggle of coming to terms with the melancholia of urban and personal lost futures alike, with his several bands mapping onto the corresponding phases of grief.

In getting to grips with Brannon's singular body of work, we might also look to Frederic Jameson's idea of the "political unconscious," which suggests that works of art are expressions of social problems that the artists themselves may not directly identify. Thus, Jameson tells us that the critic's job is to trace back from the work to the underlying political or social problem they attempt to "solve," or at least raise up to consciousness and address. In that spirit, we can ask the question: What was Brannon grieving, exactly? Perhaps his fall from grace, leaving behind the religious values of his childhood. After all, in the work of his band Laughing Hyenas, we see themes of the sacramental emerge across their discography. Or perhaps he was despairing, along with his hardcore peers, over a different loss, of one Holy Church of the Future, the promise of the Psychedelic Shack and the Fun House — Acid Detroit itself.

These days, the idea of lost futures tends to evoke images of geometric cityscapes and a life devoted primarily to leisure; indeed, this was what the progressive imaginary of high Fordism pointed to, as the Affluent Society, as it was dubbed at the time, would continue to minimize work, maximize pay and usher in the Leisure Society. Often, this loss, the sense that time has taken the wrong direction, is expressed in a backward-looking, nostalgic mode that sonically focuses on analogue synths, rudimentary drum machines, vocoders, and the whole panoply of kitsch Seventies and Eighties fetish objects and totems, the invigorating, of-its-moment futurism of the Bellville Three frozen in aspic, there to repeatedly reiterate the trajectory that neoliberalism put an end to. But the response to this destruction of working-class hopes wasn't *exclusively* expressed by self-styled futurists rejecting guitar, drums and bass, who coolly insisted on a high-tech techno future at the time. On the other side of the musical spectrum, the feverish response from suburban Reagan Youth-turned punk rockers also grappled with the No Future awaiting them, not retrospectively but imminently, as part of the unravelling fabric of their daily lives. Hardcore, whether directly political or not, expressed in real time the ripping up of the social contract that had guided the preceding thirty years.

We can also see the workings of another type of political unconscious as the Eighties began to bite and the city entered its protracted period of downturn with the Regan recession of the early Eighties, the offshoring of many jobs, the shift in manufacturing toward the Sunbelt states, and emergence of the Rust Belt — all the ways in which the decade catastrophically impacted Detroit in terms of poverty and depopulation. With no orientation toward the future and the means for collective expression being destroyed, the city began to turn in on itself, exploding in the kinds of seemingly purposeless and inchoate rage that characterizes Brannon's work. One way to illustrate this is by examining an age-old Detroit festivity.

For most of the country, October 30th is an unremarkable date that goes uncelebrated as people prepare for Halloween the next day. However, this isn't the case in Detroit. Devil's Night, a holiday traditionally characterized by relatively harmless "mischief," has instead become a night marked by intense and widespread arson around the city. For decades, Detroit police and firefighters have worked — to varying degrees of success — to prevent such riotous behavior from taking place. Reflecting the desperation of the socio-economic situation in the city, the annual acts of arson reached a fever pitch in 1984 when over four hundred fires and small blazes were set loose across Detroit, primarily in impoverished sectors of the city. On Devil's Night that year, over one thousand citizen volunteers took to the streets to monitor the arson. Additionally, for the first time since the 1967 rebellion, suburban firefighter departments rushed into the city to help quell the blazes.

In just twenty years, Detroit had gone from the booming Motor City of the 1960s to being repeatedly dubbed the "Arson and Murder Capital of America" and the "USA's Most Dangerous City," following an explosion in drug use and gang violence. This is the hellish social-economic landscape in which Detroit hardcore youth would come of age. Why wouldn't they grieve?

Stage 1: Denial

I could deny it if I liked. I could deny anything if I liked.
Oscar Wilde, *The Importance of Being Earnest*

In common with many other mythical musicians, Brannon's story starts with humble beginnings. Like Suzi Quatro of the Pleasure Seekers, Brannon grew up in Grosse Pointe, an affluent town just north of the Detroit border. His father was a minister, and the young Brannon attended church choir before opting to stay home and watch the Monkees. We will consider how this religious upbringing returns later, but for the moment, we can consider that his cutting out of church signals a certain denial of faith and death itself — a blocked spirituality, a turning away from the divine, Brannon falling from grace and walking out of Eden.

From an early age, Brannon had wanted to be a performer, taking cues from his earliest musical love, Louis Armstrong. As he got older, looking right in his backyard, Brannon knew he was destined to become a singer when he saw Detroit shock-rockers Alice Cooper, who were at this time still an arty, theatrical shock-rock troupe, not the solo musician really named Vincent Furnier. Out of this fertile ground, we get Brannon's first foray into music-making: the ultra-obscure and presumed-lost glam-punk group Static.

In Static's glam mimicry we can observe the first stage of grief — denial. Static formed in 1978 when glam's best years were still just about visible in the rear-view mirror. Glam was a phenomenon largely of the early 1970s: T. Rex's *Electric Warrior* from 1971; Bowie's *Ziggy Stardust* from 1972; the New York Dolls' self-titled album, and Alice Cooper's last great record, *Billion Dollar Babies*, in 1973. Imitating his idols like Alice Cooper, MC5, and Iggy Pop, Brannon would flail on the floor and shoot toothpaste into monitors in sync with the tune "Toothpaste and Pills," and Static is in some ways a failure or a refusal to accept the death of glam's spectacular subversion. It's idol-worship, and a denial of glam rock's falling out of relevance: Brannon has been born too late and missed his real life and true calling. Like so many other Detroit bands, Static's recordings almost vanished into the dustbin of history. There had been rumors of the legendary Static tapes in the scene for years, and Sonic Youth's Thurston Moore had begged Brannon to release them. But denial also comes with a sense of embarrassment, and Brannon was squeamish about letting anything see the light of day. In fact, he had tried to hide the band, considering it a skeleton in his closet. Had it not been for Brannon finding the lost recordings *literally* in a closet and Detroit label Third Man Records reissuing the salvaged demos and bootlegged performances on the 2021 release *Toothpaste and Pills,* they most certainly would have never surfaced. Therefore, it is only once he has worked through all the stages of his grief that glam can return both in his later bands and in the re-issue of Static's music itself.

First, though, we have to work through the anger.

Stage 2: Anger

Hate is a bottomless cup; I will pour and pour.

Euripides

If punk can be seen as a response to rock's softness, then Detroit hardcore can be seen as a response to punk's softness. While California's beach scenes may be able to lay claim to developing the *sound* of hardcore punk, they lacked the ethos of community and solidarity that Detroit intrinsically embodied. Indeed, in his oral history of Detroit hardcore, *Why Be Something That You're Not: Detroit Hardcore 1979-1985*, Tony Rettman asserts that the Detroit scene "cultivated the music's grassroots aesthetic before most cultural hot spots around the globe even knew what the music was about." Despite the rough conditions Detroit offered up at this time, we yet again see a sense of Eno's *scenius* emerging amongst the rubble.

No band exemplifies the philosophy of speed intrinsic to Detroit's hardcore scene better than Brannon's second band, the seminal group Negative Approach. Moving through denial into anger, Brannon shaved his head, shedding his glam past in favor of a new militancy, entering and eventually becoming the kingpin of the Detroit hardcore punk scene. The headquarters for Detroit hardcore were the DIY venues the Freezer and the Clubhouse. Here, marginalized, disaffected suburbanites would congregate to slam dance, stage dive, and act the fool on weekends. The scene received validation from Minor Threat's Ian MacKaye, who produced a record by the band Necros (originally from Ohio but heavily associated with the Detroit scene) and endorsed the city's unique brand of hardcore cacophony, while visits from bands like Black Flag and Bad Brains provided further inspiration.

Negative Approach — easily the best band in the scene — were true to their name, with Brannon drawing inspiration directly from bands he hated. Having clung on to something positive and drawn on the bands he loved — Alice Cooper in Static — only to discover time has in fact pulled these beloved objects from his grasp, there was nothing left for Brannon to embrace but the negative. There is no sense in which the later band is an extension or reworking of his previous musical interests — in Negative Approach, Brannon obliterates any trace of his glam persona in favor of uncompromising, unfiltered rage. It's in his rejection and almost masochistic denial of his own attachments, in what Mark Fisher would call a spirit of "nihilation" toward everything around him, that Branon helped to create something new.

Negative Approach cultivated a punishing sound that might best be described as a sonic blitz. This is best exemplified on their seminal 1981 self-titled 7" record. Clocking in ten tracks in nine minutes, the influential recording contains some of hardcore punk's earliest anthems like the raging "Nothing," a song that captures the themes that would dominate Brannon's life, art, and psyche. "Nothing" also captures the mingling of the personal and political, the social and psychological:

You try to make things work and gain something
It's all no use, it's all worth nothing
Complete satisfaction, too impossible to believe
Nothing's ever fucking gonna work for me

Tomorrow seems so hopeless
Can't keep it off my mind
Another day of nothing I'm running out of time
I've got nothing I can look forward to

I'm always left with nothing
I'm always told things I don't want to hear
My destiny's become quite clear

Life's never fucking given nothing to me
It's just stood by and watched me bleed
Tomorrow seems so hopeless
Can't keep it off my mind
Another day of nothing I'm running out of time

Brannon is also responsible for a phrase that became in some ways the slogan of the entire Detroit scene: "Why Be Something That You're Not?" In the moment, Brannon couldn't have foreseen in writing such songs that he, a skinhead punk railing against the psychic damage of the monotony of suburban hegemony and urban decay, would become, as he later quipped, "the Francis Scott Key of hardcore." With tracks like the nine-second "Pressure," Negative Approach pushed song length and musical speed to its logical end point of hyper-compression. What we see here is acceleration as a desperate lunge for an exit. Negative Approach play so fast that time seems to collapse in on itself, and in that temporal breakdown perhaps an escape route will emerge.

However, just as *Two Lane Blacktop*'s final conflagration reminds us, an addiction to speed is an unsustainable strategy for the long term. Before the release of their landmark 1983 LP *Tied Down*, Negative Approach had already burnt out, leaving Brannon to scour the depths of depression, epitomized by the music of his next band, one of Detroit's greatest and most overlooked.

Stages 3 and 4: Bargaining and Depression

Depression is, after all and above all, a theory about the world, about life.

Mark Fisher, *Ghosts of My Life*

BRANNON: *I'm glad we have this outlet because I hate to think what we'd be doing if we weren't playing music. I just, I don't know.*

INTERVIEWER: *You don't seem like particularly evil people, though.*

BRANNON: *You don't know us very well.*

With Negative Approach already behind him before the release of their debut full-length, Brannon — never one to look back for too long — formed a new group with his housemates. The new band featured a driving, pulsing rhythm section of bassist Kevin Strickland and drummer Jim Kimball. Rounding out the new group's explosive-chaotic sound was Larissa Strickland, formerly of post-punk band L-Seven (not to be confused with the grunge-metal group L7). An important Detroit band in their own right, L-Seven made jerky, frenetic post-punk, earning them the opportunity to open for the Birthday Party. Attending the show, Brannon — seeing Nick Cave's vampiric mane — was inspired to change musical directions and regrow his hair. If we are to think of this moment in Brannon's career as representative of bargaining, we can read this decision to grow out his hair as a compromise. Sure, he can't be Alice Cooper or Iggy Pop anymore, but he can still have long hair. After all, is goth rock not an update on glam for the undead Reagan years? Further still, long hair in the 1960s was a key signifier of counterculture and communist ideals.

Formed out of ashes and a will to experiment, the new group's naïveté begot a certain intensity and unorthodoxy that would go on to earn them the reverence of indie giants like Nirvana, Mudhoney, and Sonic Youth. They were none other than the caustic, tortured Laughing Hyenas.

Laughing Hyenas debuted on Touch and Go Records with 1987's, Butch Vig-produced *Merry-Go-Round*. The album is a return to the Stooges' circus of pleasures, only to find the candy-colored tents abandoned. If — as discussed in the previous section on techno — Detroit is haunted by the stain of place and the overflowing of time, then it is fitting that Laughing Hyenas' onslaught begins with the track entitled "Stain." Setting up the core theme of the Laughing Hyenas' musical output, "Stain" appropriately begins their career with Brannon first muttering, then howling, "Been a sinner all my life, but that you already know," and climaxes with him repeating, seemingly *ad infinitum*, "I'm coming down." After the high rage and sheer velocity of Negative Approach comes the sinking into depletion, fatigue, remorse. Mark Fisher reminds us in his essay on Joy Division, a band who we'll consider in tandem with the Hyenas later, that "Speed is a connectivity drug, a drug that made sense of a world in which electronic connections were madly proliferating. But the comedown is vicious."

Two years later, the band released their most abrasive record, 1989's *You Can't Pray a Lie*, again produced by "Nirvana man" Butch Vig. Once again — from just the title alone — we ought to note a sacramental element permeating *You Can't Pray a Lie*, which tints the songs like stained glass with themes of Christian religiosity. The cover art, depicting a female icon with her eyes raised up to heaven, drives home this theme. As a testament to their partiality for the biblical, take the record's crushing closer track, "New Gospel," in which Brannon pleads for understanding, singing, "I only wanted to do what I thought was right." Despite Brannon's desire to absolve sins, it seems he is damned nonetheless, locked into a Sisyphean cycle of struggle. He can temporarily banish the ghosts, but he knows they will return. Larissa's guitar surges and scratches through the mix while the Hyenas' rhythm section hits harder than ever. Brannon's vocals are devoid of melody, purely focused on establishing a new high/low in throat-shredding brutality.

By this point in the Hyenas' career, it was clear that an essential component of their sound derived from an emphasis on bass. While Detroit garage punk groups like the Gories and the White Stripes, who we'll look at later, forego bass altogether, the Hyenas let Kevin Strickland's bass propel their songs forward. With bass clearly dominating in the mix, it gives guitarist Larissa the space to add noisy, feedback-drenched riffs, which complement and color tracks like a painter adding the finishing textural strokes on a canvas. Bass is of course the foundational instrument of funk, clearly linked to Detroit's premiere collective Parliament-Funkadelic, and the grounding grooves of bass would also become a central sonic element in techno and rave culture, anchoring the psychedelic dance music to Earth, returning us to the Fun House and Psychedelic Shack. Bass isn't a key instrument in hardcore punk though, and what the predominance of bass does is align the Laughing Hyenas more with post-punk's dub and funk-influenced bands like Public Image Limited, the Clash, and the Pop Group, rather than garage rock. However, nowhere is the similarity in driving bass ethos and the attempt to exorcise depression clearer than in another band directly influenced by Brannon's hero and art-rock godfather Iggy Pop — Joy Division.

Across the Atlantic, a scrappy band of Mancunian schoolboys had turned onto the proto-punk sounds of Detroit, worshipping MC5 and the Stooges. According to the band's bassist Peter Hook, it was their lead singer Ian Curtis — who initially learned of Pop through his wife Deborah — that introduced his bandmates to Iggy. Though they famously formed in the aftermath of an early Sex Pistols gig, seeing Iggy Pop with David Bowie on keyboards at the Apollo in 1977 was equally eye-opening. After all, the first incarnation of their band was named Warsaw, taken from an icy instrumental track off of Bowie's *Low*. Eventually calling themselves Joy Division, they would go on to lay the groundwork for goth rock by combining the raw power of Pop's earlier Stooges era with the atmosphere of his arty Berlin records.

The overlaps between Detroit and Manchester, the complex back-and-forth between European avant-garde and the Stooges, Iggy and punk, post-punk and Joy Division, is found, as I will argue later, in its most surprising and immediate form later with the rapper Danny Brown. Yet it is there too in the work of Laughing Hyenas. We might even think of Laughing Hyenas as the Detroit equivalent of Joy Division — there are many visual, sonic and thematic analogues between the two, ostensibly rather different, groups.

Joy Division were formed in an industrial landscape of factories and smoke, against the brutalist backdrop of Manchester — a city that C.P. Lee described as "generated by the future, visions of the future" — now degraded, dirtied and shifting into post-industrial decline; a grimy, boring city where the prospect of advancing in society was nearly non-existent. In Manchester, the defining feeling was one of boredom and mundane toil, which gave way to a certain mania on the weekends. Similarly, in Otto Buj's 2021 documentary film, *The Real and Imagined History of Detroit Hardcore*, Brannon described Detroit as a place where there was nothing but "dope, hookers, and pavement." The names of both bands echo each other, conjoining laughter and joy with something rigid and militaristic, feral and animalistic. It's also worth noting the way the band names bleed into the performances of their respective frontmen. Curtis suffered from epilepsy, his struggle within his own body giving Joy Division's performances a sense of the dangerously, disturbingly embattled, always on the precipice of ending in collapse. Meanwhile, Brannon lurches, scowling and roaring as he skulks around the stage channeling a loose, primal rage more akin to the half-pained, half-ecstatic, cathartic scream that segues "T.V. Eye" into "Loose" on the Stooges' *Fun House*.

Discussing Joy Division in *Ghosts of My Life*, Fisher suggests that, "because Joy Division's bleakness was without any specific cause, they crossed the line from the blue of sadness into the black of depression," and I would suggest the same is true of the Hyenas. Though the bands don't sound similar, and their respective producers Butch Vig and Martin Hannett — while epochal production wizards of their respective eras — have very different approaches, and Curtis and Brannon are worlds apart as vocalists, it is important to note, within the specifics of differing times and spaces, the ways they similarly constitute art and expression. Laughing Hyenas and Joy Division express the same underlying ethos: a struggle with depression. The lyrics to Negative Approach's "Nothing" are an expression not just of unknown pleasures, but of utterly inconceivable ones. For a direct example of how Brannon and Curtis were suffering along similar lines, let us examine two uncannily intertwined lyrics:

Tomorrow seems so hopeless, Can't keep it off my mind, Another day of nothing...

Negative Approach, "Nothing"

Looked beyond the day in hand, there's nothing there at all...
Joy Division, "Twenty Four Hours"

It's also instructive to examine the covers of the bands' masterpiece records: *Unknown Pleasures* and *Life of Crime*. Faceless, nameless, calculated, and modernist — these adjectives come to mind when gazing upon *Unknown Pleasures*' Peter Savile-designed cover, which has achieved iconic status. There's an anonymity here that hints at the depression sufferer's desire to disappear, to render oneself imperceptible; to "Remember Nothing" and exist in the realm of mere "Shadowplay."

While there is a certain cosmic coldness to Joy Division's imagery, the songs themselves are often tormented by loss and the unbridgeable abyss between people, between the object and desire. Further, *Unknown Pleasures*' cover — simply a textbook-ripped graph of a pulsar's radio emission — signals at a cold rationality, a scientific precision, and men who knew too much. Fisher reminds us that Joy Division were presenting the final, unvarnished truth of life. Meanwhile, *Life of Crime*'s stark black-and-white cover, depicting a heart shot through with arrows, is cartoonish and hints at the grotesque. It's unapologetically DIY, speaking to the group's artistic ethos and sensibility. If *Unknown Pleasures* could be an electric reading of depressive brainwaves, then *Life of Crime* represents the emotional toil of battling against depression. The bleeding heart, pierced, struggling to empathize and feel love.

While Curtis' vocals are non-blues, flattish, affectless, numbed but needful, Brannon's remarkable voice is located somewhere on the other side, *beyond* blues. If "grain" in voice — the raspiness and throatiness we associate with rock and blues — reflects an intrusion of the body into the otherwise disembodied realm of pure voice, reminding us of both our and the singer's sensual and suffering materiality,

Brannon's is, by conventional standards, disconcertingly, unpleasantly raw, pushing us past pleasure and into the realm of the abject, a theme that Brannon also carries forward into his lyrics.

Indeed, *Life of Crime* epitomizes everything that made them heroes in the eyes of their peers. We can look to the record's promethean opener "Everything I Want" for proof. Beginning with Larissa's hissing feedback and a calm-before-the-storm bass lick, "Everything I Want" erupts like a pipe-bomb into an explosive, barely controlled chaos. Waiting in the wings, Brannon enters with his characteristically impassioned vocals. Dropping us directly into the pit of depression with life-or-death stakes, Brannon laments:

Today might be my last as far as I can see
When everything I need
Everything I want
Is so far out of reach

The scorching, suicidal opener sets the tone for what's to follow: an eight-song slab of soul-bearing hardcore. On the album's magnetic centerpiece "Here We Go Again," we're thrust into the endless, unfolding cycle of dissatisfaction that comes with the Hyenas' collective life of drugs, crime, and poverty. With the lines, "I can't remember when / Refresh my memory if you can / Was the last time we were satisfied? / Couldn't stay away if we tried", "Here We Go Again" illustrates the feedback loop that comes with the conditioning of drug abuse.

The music of both Joy Division and the Hyenas is a response to a totalizing sense of No Future that creates all-encompassing depression. There is no way out. All that's left is to continually search for the unknown pleasures that come with a life of crime. While Brannon and Larissa fled Detroit to Ann Arbor, where they would raid frat houses for food, Curtis fled not only his hometown of Macclesfield and the musical hotbed of Manchester, but his entire Earthly existence.

Two years later, the Hyenas tapped into the peak of their powers and plumbed the depths of despair with their 1992 EP *Crawl*. *Crawl* finds the group retaining the brutality of *Life of Crime* but moving into the blues-inspired dirges that would characterize 1995's *Hard Times*. Perhaps the most compelling song in the group's catalog, the EP opens with the track it was named after. Trapped in hell, living in darkness, "Crawl" erupts with the confession, "I wanna live forever," and ends with Brannon screaming repeatedly, "Crawl on the floor!" This image, Brannon on the floor of a church pew, on the brink, begging for immortality, shifts from being haunting to disturbing, given the severity with which he delivers his sermon. It's difficult not to contrast the lithe pleasure-bound writhing on the stage that Iggy and Brannon in his younger day's aspired to with the act of painfully crawling toward a distant — perhaps non-existent — salvation. Both men are on the floor, but while Pop was luxuriating in it, Brannon seems to be anguished as he collapses to the ground, still confessing, "Been a sinner all my life…"

Crawl sounds like a group of musicians on the brink, and it's a miracle to think that the band survived this period, with the potential for death via hard drugs or suicide. Indeed, three years later they would sing, "Looking back now girl, it's a wonder that we're still alive."

Stage 5: Acceptance

After years of influencing important bands, surviving the rise and fall of grunge, never even approaching a song that sounded like a hit or landing a major record deal, the uncompromising Laughing Hyenas entered the studio for one last swing on 1995's bluesy swan song *Hard Times*. With a professional album cover that makes it look like this might be the group's attempt at hitting the bigtime, it's unsurprising that on *Hard Times* we find Larissa embracing more electric rock 'n roll riffs and Brannon a bluesier croon. The result is that the band — for the first and only time in their career — sound more the Rolling Stones than the Stooges.

With its dark blue album sleeve, *Hard Times*' artwork is indicative of the album's unabashed blues influences. After all, what are the blues if not the musical equivalent of a prayer? Sadness and confession set to song, often with a tongue-in-cheek wink and laugh at the absurdity of it all? Indeed, the blues is a kind of mournful adaptation of spirituals, and has always had a rich back-and-forth and intermingling with gospel music. If Laughing Hyenas represent Brannon's grief moving through bargaining to depression, then it's fitting that *Hard Times* corresponds to this stage's totality washing over the group with the first glimmers of acceptance. The sentiment they seem to be sharing this time around is, "Yeah, we can't win, but at least we're having fun losing."

Interestingly, following in the footsteps of Norman Whitfield, and in marked contrast to the hyper-compression of Negative Approach, *Hard Times* finds the group unconcerned with time. Repeatedly, they allow dirge-like jams to crack six minutes in length: "Hard Times Blues" 7:20; "Stay" 7:58; "Slump" 6:15; "Each Dawn I Die" 6:27. The Hyenas were certainly a band who never put limitations on themselves. Acclimated to living in darkness, accustomed to sinking into the syrupy depths of lethargy and numbness, *Hard Times* is an exercise in sedation, even featuring a brooding, drunk-sounding cover of Johnny Cash's "Home of the Blues." Indeed, by this point, Brannon had become Detroit's Man in Black, a figure of sorrow who rallies for those "whose bad trip left them cold."

But *Hard Times* is also shot through with a certain optimism that suggests a light at the end of the tunnel. Take for example the album's closing track, "Each Dawn I Die," which tell its listener that despite living in a purgatorial hellscape, you will wake up in the morning. It's no coincidence the song's title was taken from the name of a 1939 gangster film, which centers around a falsely imprisoned man. Indeed, the sentiment of *Hard Times* seems to suggest that, if one puts in their time and waits out their darkest nights, dawn will eventually arrive. Every dawn may be a little death, but ultimately, we're still alive. Of course, this is a uniquely Detroit sense of perseverance, as the city and its residents are associated with an unbreakable spirit for a reason. Indeed, if Brannon three years earlier had been vocalizing his depression's rock-bottom on *Crawl*, the living in darkness seemed to be ending. The band would dissolve after *Hard Times*, but tragically, the story doesn't end there.

In 2006, aged forty-six, Larissa Strickland would pass away from an alleged overdose of the prescription drug Xanax. I'd like to take advantage of the space afforded me here to bestow some much deserved praise upon her. Larissa was — by every measure — a guitar goddess. She carried the torch, descending from Detroit's lineage of revolutionary players: Kramer, Asheton, and "Sonic" Smith. When many thought there was nowhere left for guitar players to go, Larissa plunged into uncharted territory. A master of controlled feedback and head-splitting noise, she was a tour de force that ought to be placed in the pantheon of musical greats.

Let the Good Times Roll

In 1970, the original shock-rockers, Detroit's Alice Cooper, released their LP *Easy Action*. Nearly thirty years later, John Brannon would reappropriate that title as the name of his new band. Formed in 1997, Easy Action synthesizes Static's glam-rock swagger, Negative Approach's hardcore punk riffage, and Laughing Hyenas' appetite for destruction. This is reflected in both of their records — 2001's self-titled debut and 2005's *Friends of Rock & Roll*. Tracks like "You and Me" and "What's the Deal" burn with a hard-rock fire and, though they retain a hardcore punch, are informed by the work of glam-rockers like Cooper, who had a knack for writing a killer chorus. On "Friends of Rock & Roll," Brannon is ready to have some fun and do as he pleases, bellowing out:

> We walk the streets at night, the city looks in fear
> Do what the fuck we want, wanna make it clear.

Here, the depression and rage has faded, and the good times have begun.

The final stage of grief is acceptance. And Easy Action certainly reads as a sort of coming to terms with what was lost. The ghost of Alice Cooper haunts the band, but there is no self-deception here. Brannon is no longer glammed up and shooting toothpaste into monitors, trying to convince us that glam is still alive. The disaffected Reagan-era rage of Negative Approach is now channeled into brilliant hooks and killer howls. Perhaps Brannon's early experiments with Negative Approach were an attempt to give him the sufficient velocity to traverse the long, dark night that was awaiting him, and perhaps only a city as devoted to speed and acceleration as Detroit could have given him that impetus to break on through to the other side. Detroit's doubleness returns, both the problem and the solution. The depression of Laughing Hyenas has been replaced with a certain dark joy, a love for music-making and a knowing black-humor. Brannon had exorcized his ghosts, acclimated to the darkness, and is now free of the haunted lost object. Freed from anger and agitation, he is finally capable, as the band name tells us, of some *easy* action, covering Seventies glam icons like Roxy Music and Cheap Trick.

Throughout it all, Brannon remained committed to a belief in a better world, an alternative to the order of things. Across his four-decade career, he could be spotted repping a White Panther Party T-shirt, which we will recall was one of Detroit's earliest countercultural revolutionary groups. Clearly, this is a reminder and signifier of the radical disavowal, dissident energy, and collectivism that must be tapped back into if we are to build a better world.

What we ultimately see in Brannon's journey through the dark night is the possibility of moving through. Throughout his musical career, we find him wrestling with the notion of being caught in repetitions and cycles. In order to work through such a compulsion to repeat, we find art not for art's sake, but the role that art plays for many: *art for survival's sake*. Or rather, *art for sanity's sake*. While the world was trying to shut out the viability of community, the Detroit hardcore circuit carved out a space for recreating the conditions of group healing and therapy. Like Detroit's gospel churches, Brannon's bands and local scenes recreated the conditions of collective ritual, fervor, and ecstasy. The ballad of John Brannon raises the question: What should be available to all in the utopian post-capitalist city-to-come? Certainly, if in the example of the Laughing Hyenas — one group among the many who found salvation in a scene and in the catharsis of art — teaches us anything, it's the necessity of the time and space to communally heal the wounds of a damaged life.

6. TIME OUT OF JOINT: MICK COLLINS, GARAGE-PUNK REVIVALISTS AND J DILLA

In the early 1990s, after the collapse of the Soviet Union and the "triumph" of Western capitalism over the whole of Europe, Francis Fukuyama observed that society had entered what he called "the End of History." In *Ghosts of My Life*, Fisher characterizes this unipolar period as one in which — borrowing from Derrida borrowing from Hamlet — there is a pervasive sense that "the time is out of joint." Nowhere, I'd argue, is this temporal dislocation felt so profoundly as in Detroit — we only need to point to the population collapse and the physical devastation wrought on the city, outlined in the previous chapter, to see this. In response to this experience of disordered time, of the future as a nothing where something should be, many musicians in Detroit took on new strategies around rhythm and a certain, perhaps inevitable, element of retrospection began to take hold.

Grappling with what's appropriate to the times is fundamental to the ethos of the Gories, and their main man Mick Collins, as well as their successors the White Stripes. It also informs the great creative genius of hip-hop maestro J Dilla. Both Dilla and the garage rockers were working, in a sense, with and against tradition, creating music that is filled with eerie absences and weird counter-presences. Lopsided and off-kilter, their music opens up new spaces either between guitar and drums or between beats, messing with predictable dynamics and the reliability, regularity, metronomic, and measured pleasure principle of *groove*.

If time *is* somehow out of joint, the question arises whether this dislocation has come about by accident or is the result of an affront. With both comes trauma, and it's important once again to recognize the pace at which Detroit goes from being the birthplace of the defining Fordist social contract, home of some of the great jewels of twentieth-century American culture, to — as it was dubbed in the Nineties — "America's first third-world city." We might consider how this gives an odd, vertiginous, two-fold temporality to daily life, a paradoxical combination of simultaneously accelerating while also slamming to a halt. To visualize this idea, we might imagine how, if a car jams on the brakes, everything in the backseat is flung forward, and consider the Nineties as the point when time hits the brakes and suddenly the past is hurled violently forward, into the present. Such a sudden brake check would make anyone a little woozy.

Stuck in Thee Garage

Rich Tupica: What used to piss the Gories off at shows?

Mick Collins: One thing we couldn't abide was when an out-of-town band came into town and thought they were better than Detroit. We just couldn't abide it. On a couple of occasions, that happened. We were like, "Alright, we're going to teach you a lesson tonight."

It's a warm August evening in 2021, and I'm at Mexicantown's premiere venue El Club for what's slated to be a particularly special gig. With a whole week of shows, the venue, located on the southwest side of the city, is celebrating its triumphant return from the COVID-19 lockdown. Tonight, the show is packed to the brim with eager people, and is certainly close to being sold out. The audience spans generations: wide-eyed kids from the local garage rock scene, millennial hipsters with thick-rimmed glasses clutching a craft beer, and older scene veterans repping Stooges T-shirts from their glory days. You'd think a pretty special touring act is in town, but you'd be wrong. The talent is all local.

Opening the show are current kings of the scene, the electrifying torchbearers of Detroit garage rock, the Stools — Will Lorenz, Krystian Quint, and Charles Stahl. The trio launch into their usual brand of high-velocity, turbo-charged bluesy punk, which mainly captivates the group of early twenty-somethings who know full well the opener is worth catching. After the Stools finish, the floor feels charged with electricity as it fills up with the rest of the attendees, who until now have been smoking cigarettes out on the patio and drinking beers barside. As the space reaches capacity, a sort of transcendent energy fills the venue. Looking around, you'd be right to think that headliner the Gories are one of the most beloved bands in the city, because they are. But it wasn't always this way. In fact, when the trio — Danny Kroha, Mick Collins, and Peggy O'Neil — started back in the late 1980s, they were hardly paid any attention to. Back in those early days, when they were acknowledged, it was largely with a feeling of distaste, and — like many disruptive bands who came before them — they had beer bottles hurled at them. Not that this ever stopped them. Like the Detroit musicians who came before them, the Gories stuck to a heedless commitment to self-expression, regardless of reception. Now, three decades later, the tides of history have turned as they prepare to take their place on the throne.

The Gories take to the stage and are met with an overwhelming applause from the whole club, but especially the Gen-Z attendees upfront. The high energy is immediately evident. Launching into "Feral" from their classic 1989 record *Houserockin'*, the crowd explodes into a head-bobbing frenzy, jumping to the explosive drum beat. The group marches along, and by the time they get to another signature track, "Detroit Breakdown" (a track updating and geographically recentering Doctor Ross's 1953 tune "Chicago Breakdown"), the crowd of kids have broken out into a classic Detroit mosh pit, a secret dance of the punks that feeds off of a certain combination of chaos, solidarity, and love. Collins confesses to the crowd that he "never thought we'd see moshing at a Gories show!" Indeed, watching the crowd of young folks shouting out song requests and dancing their asses off to what was once a neglected Detroit band, we momentarily swim through the electric haze into an alternate timeline. I catch myself thinking, *here it is*, time has caught up with itself.

What does this mean, to have time catch up with itself? To answer that we might recall that Detroit is a city marked by a certain degree of insularity. The city's people champion their own, and there's a special sense of supporting those who have stayed, making themselves a fixture in the locale. In a city where there seems to be every impetus to get out, there is a unification amongst those who have remained. Indeed, for those who have held steadfast to Detroit, there's a special sense of cross-generational solidarity that pervades the punk rock dive bars and clubs.

To make that more concrete, we can look to both the history of Detroit's population collapse and the ways in which it radically changes the ethnic composition of the city, a process that was well underway by the mid-Nineties and has only just begun to reverse in the past few years. In 1950, Detroit's population peaked at 1,850,000, making it the fourth biggest city in the USA. Over the next seventy years, that figure would drop to a 2020 low of 639,000, consistently losing between one hundred to three hundred thousand residents per decade. This represents, in total, a 65% decline. The percentage of black residents went from 16% in 1950 to 70% in 2020, making Detroit a majority black city. A large part of the population loss and the resulting economic decline was due to white flight — the white population dropped from 83% in 1950 to 10% in 2020, and this exodus, coupled with deindustrialization and corporate abandonment, produced an unparalleled collapse in the tax base, eventually leading to the bankruptcy of the city in 2013, the largest ever municipal bankruptcy in US history. Many people got out, but for those who didn't, there is a unique distillation of a particular history, commitment, tenacity, and sense of shared struggle and release.

With vehicles obviously being central to the history, culture and philosophy of Detroit, there's something uniquely appropriate about *garage* rock playing such a big role in the music of the city. After all, what is a garage? A designated space to store cars, and with garage rock, we see this usually static space now repurposed for kinetic music-making, sweeping us away to distant places, and given the city's fame as Motor City, there is an irony in that Detroit musicians rarely ever go out on tour or even play outside the city. As the Dirtbombs, a Mick Collins band we'll discuss further later, sing on track eight of their 2003 record *Dangerous Magical Noise*, there is a sense that Detroit musicians are "Stuck in Thee Garage." *Thee* garage. Detroit is thee garage of America, the place from which garage rock originates and to which, if it ever left, it would return. But given it's already in the Mecca, where else is there to go?

With Detroit musicians often not traveling or hitting the road, there isn't always a sense of career progression, but there is a sense of contributing to a presiding spirit of the city. As a result, a nucleus of creativity forms, and there is a unique sense of inserting oneself into a secret lineage and legacy. The garage that is Detroit has produced its own musical language, heroes, scenes, and even classic record canon. In the age of the internet, it's easy to let the media impose a canonized set of classic records which erases local specificities. But Detroit rejects this, instead opting to have its own canon, chosen because they shaped the city's history: *Fun House, Cloud Nine, Enter, Night Moves, Tied Down*, to name only a few that we've already discussed. There's an immediacy, history, and legacy that comes with a record like the Dirtbombs' *Ultraglide in Black* or — to set up another band that we will also discuss at greater length later — the White Stripes, with their fan favorite *De Stijl*. In Detroit, the notion that we are simply handed down a certain list of cultural objects that we must respect is never really acknowledged, at least in terms of music culture.

While there might be something quintessentially Detroit about garage rock, the Gories' first album, the legendary *Houserockin'*, taps into a somewhat different ethos. The garage is a suburban, middle-class phenomena, a space that became available for the kids who had them, and while it is now just a genre tag, it was once the existence of these spaces within a more affluent but boring suburbia of the 1950s and 1960s that made the formation of such bands possible. Iggy, we'll recall, didn't have the space to practice his drums, so his parents let him move into the bedroom. Suburbia and mass production created the conditions: the boredom, the practice space, and the relatively cheap instruments and equipment that allowed a new genre to emerge. The Gories represent a different legacy: practice sessions and shows played in houses and basements where official venues aren't available or are too expensive. As the title of the album suggests, the Gories belong to the tradition of the house party. Rather than garage rock, perhaps *house* rock is more fitting: rolling back the carpets, setting up the amps, inviting the neighbors over and taking advantage of an alternate infrastructure, a circle of shows and nights out based around the dwelling places of those in your friendship groups. Urban and more informal, house rock privileges informality, community energy, and enthusiasm over equipment and polish, a scene more appropriate to the Detroit of the Nineties, an extension of the idea of the Psychedelic Shack, a space of comfort, free-expression, and ease. Don't worry about getting it wrong or making a fool of yourself, you're at home!

In a revealing interview with Collins by Rich Tupica on the *Turn it Down* blog, discussing Collins' times in the Gories, the following exchange takes place:

TUPICA: Where did the Gories play at in Detroit?

COLLINS: Paychecks in Hamtramck and Reruns, which was just across the border into Dearborn. We also played a lot of house parties. Anyone that gave us $25, and/or beer got a show. The picture on the back of *Houserockin'* was taken at somebody's party. The picture on the front of *Outta Here* was taken at a community concert series at Dally in the Alley.

It's also worth noting, in order to get a further flavor of the idiosyncratic, multi-generational, and open attitude that pervades Detroit's music scene, that in one such community concert, one where anyone could sign up to play, the Gories ended up on the same bill as MC5's front man Rob Tyner, playing directly after the Detroit hero.

Time Out of Joint

One of the most interesting and unusual elements of the Gories' sound and set up is that they don't have a bass player, and nor of course do the great overground ambassadors of Detroit garage, the White Stripes.

This rejection of bass is in some ways a direct act of sacrilege, a conscious rejection of the city's history, while at the same time foraging through its past for a new one. Perhaps desecration is a better term, given the fact that bass is of course the foundational instrument of funk, and would go on to become a central sonic element in techno and rave culture. Yet, the influence and essential nature of bass goes even further back in the story of Detroit's musical legacy, as the city was responsible for raising the most influential jazz bassist of all time — Paul Chambers. Chambers' reliably creative bass grooves would earn him the opportunity to cut records with all of the greats of his day: Bill Evans, Red Garland, Chet Baker, Sonny Clarke, Cannonball Adderley, Thelonious Monk, Hank Mobley, and so many more. Not only that, both John Coltrane and Miles Davis would enlist Chambers in their bands. Thus, Chambers' bouncing bass can be heard on genre-defining records such as Miles' *Kind of Blue* and *Sketches of Spain*, as well as Coltrane's *Blue Train, Giant Steps*, and *A Love Supreme*.

If the Laughing Hyenas foregrounded bass by looking to near-contemporaneous post-punk and goth, the garage scene of the Nineties, with its bassless acts like the Hentchmen and Bantam Rooster, produced a music that is profoundly out of joint. With the absence of the rhythmic fullness and regular pulse that keeps the listener unconsciously locked into a song's groove, garage rockers find themselves trying to unite elements in the face of a missing link. What emerges is a way of readjusting to and recomposing the elements of the song, aiming for the same affects, addressing the urge to party and get the house rockin' in a strange, new, misaligned musical space where something is missing. How can you still have a good time when something so fundamental has been lost? Many bands are anti-commercial and produce work no major company would look at, but few have been more committed to anti-cooptation than the Gories, who attempt to blend a studied anti-commercialism with the creation of a new set of sonic coordinates and signifiers. Central to their ethos is the desire have a good time, to give rock thrills, but by different means, in an unbalanced and less predictable age. Can we still rock when something elemental is missing? Can we find thrills and excitement when the future has disappeared? Can we still gather together and dance now? It may have taken thirty years for it to be fully appreciated, but as the crowd at El Club testifies, the Gories' answer is a fierce yes.

New ways but the love stays.

Detroit in the Nineties

If any piece of media best captures the city in this time of garage rockers and hip-hoppers, it is Anthony Drazan's 1992 film *Zebrahead*, a Romeo-and-Juliet romance set in Detroit. The story follows a white Jewish teenager named Zack, Z for short, who has fallen for Nikki, a black girl and cousin of his best friend Dee. Rather than having two royal families, the feud and central tension of the film is one of crossing the black and white divide. When Z reveals his honest intentions to Dee, he is supportive of his friend. The boys care about each other deeply, and look out for each other whilst navigating thorny instances of racial division at school. Though some students have some snarky comments, the inseparable duo never let the disses get to them. Ultimately, when violence strikes in the form of a school bully who can't bear the thought of Z and Nikki's relationship, Dee takes a bullet for Z in the emotional climax of the film. Thus, unlike Eminem's *8 Mile* of the same era, *Zebrahead* sincerely champions interracial friendship and love, as well as cultural appreciation and exchange.

The film is also a revealing portrait of the city at that time. Driving scenes around burned-out Detroit in Z's jeep are set to hip-hop blasting from the radio, capturing the juxtaposition between the eerily abandoned and just-holding-on, even thriving neighborhoods. The film also showcases some shots of the Detroit People Mover, the above-ground automated tram, in all its glory.

Another way *Zebrahead* represents the city is by also being grounded in music. As critic Marc Savlov of the *Austin Chronicle* noted, "The pulsing beats collected by music supervisor M.C. Serch ... act almost as another living player in the film, imbuing it with a certitude which surely would have left Drazan's film lacking had it not been there." Zack's chauvinistic single father runs a failing jazz and soul record shop, which serves as an alternative form of education for Z, who harbors a love for DJing. The film also foreshadows the arrival of the legendary Detroit musician we will turn to next. In a scene during recess, Z is conducting a breakbeat-driven DJ set when — in a nod to the film's classic, Shakespearian set-up — he overlays the isolated funk break with a choral Puccini record, demonstrating to his love interest Nikki that "you can sample anything." Anything, indeed. As we will see with the crate-digging king J Dilla, a sample can come from anywhere, in an increasingly looped, non-linear and out-of-joint musical space-time.

Donuts: J Dilla's Wounded Temporality

TUPICA: *Back in Eighties, how did you hear the rare records that influenced the Gories?*

MICK COLLINS: *It wasn't rare in Detroit. Everyone talks about that stuff being rare, they weren't in Detroit. Those records cost a quarter. Everyone you knew had all those records. What would happen would be someone would discover a record that they paid a dime or quarter for somewhere. Within ten days they had played it for everyone, and everyone could buy one because they were so cheap and easily available. Then we go to a different city and find out these records were impossible to get and cost a fortune.*

J Dilla is the exemplary hip-hop artist of this moment, primarily in that he mastered crate-digging, the art of recycling the past, in order to generate new, unprecedented possibilities. The hardcore punk kids had attempted to escape through acceleration, but this hadn't proven a viable technique for fleeing the crushing weight of the present. If the road ahead was blocked, then perhaps a different tactic was required. Dilla's rhythmic strategy is to try and wrongfoot time, throw it off balance, and set it moving again, to jolt it out of stasis and back into the groove. Like how 'ardkore and junglist artists in the UK at this time were using programmed rhythms to create previously impossible percussive flurries, foregrounding drums and stretching time to engender a rhythmic psychedelia, Dilla was also creating his own.

While techno was ubiquitous amongst Detroit's black population in the 1980s, a minority of listeners were also picking up on another emerging black popular music coming from New York City — hip-hop. Pioneered by party DJs spinning looped breakbeats while a master of ceremonies kept the party alive, hip-hop emerged as a form of music that naturally cross-pollinated with politics, socialization, and street fashion. One key player was DJ Kool Herc. Herc's "merry-go-round" technique developed out of mixing between records, forming the bedrock of DJ culture.

Back in Detroit, the hip-hop scene was relatively sparse.

Beyond important DJs the Electrifyin' Mojo and Ken Collier, Jeff "the Wizard" Mills, who we've already discussed in chapter four, was championing this breakbeat-driven music from the East Coast. It's no surprise, then, that Mills' seminal techno collective Underground Resistance was largely influenced by hip-hop's streetwise ethos and hard-hitting beats. While Detroit techno producers used drum machines and sequencers to produce tracks that sounded as frictionless as possible, James Dewitt Yancey — better known as J Dilla — would use those same synthetic tools to express a different and more dislocated sensibility.

In his 2022 book *Dilla Time*, Dan Charnas traces the life and times of the legendary Detroit producer. Central to his thesis, Charnas argues that Dilla's unique rhythms — caught somewhere between straight, swing, and syncopated — form a new conception of musical time, which he calls "Dilla Time." Before we dive further into Dilla's off-kilter sense of temporality, lets rewind the tape and first discuss Yancey's background as a young music prodigy in Detroit's Conant Gardens neighborhood.

From birth, James Yancey's parents instilled the value of music in their son. His mother — Maureen "Ma Dukes" Yancey — was an opera singer. Early on, she identified her infant son's inclination towards music, claiming he had a sense of perfect pitch before he could speak. Meanwhile, his father — Dewitt Yancey — was an upright bass player. As Charnas regales in *Dilla Time*, Dewitt would often have to play his son like a bass — plucking the baby's tummy and humming deep notes — to soothe him and stop him from crying.

While his parents' instruments represent traditional forms of black excellence, associated with a sense of social-class mobility and high culture, James would master a completely different musical language that came with its own set of cultural signifiers. The upright bass is one of the most physical instruments, and there is a strenuousness that comes with plucking away, anchoring tunes, bridging the gap between the rhythm section and melody. Indeed, one could say the bass is the most embodied instrument. While the guitarists often get the spotlight and look good, you'll often find the bassist pushed off in the corner sweating, operating deep in the groove — trying to get in the pocket — of the drummer's beats. Additionally, it is the bassist who produces the low vibrational notes that people actually feel reverberate through their bodies. What Dilla eventually did was supersede both his parents, mastering machines that would allow him to conjure up unnaturally heavy bass grooves and chopped-up vocal spots from the beyond.

In his high school years in Conant Gardens — like the Belleville Three who came before him — James would bond with two classmates, going by the stage names T3 and Baatin, over a love of music, specifically rap battle culture. With James — now going by Jay Dee — at the helm of beat production, they formed the group Slum Village. To get a sense of Jay's talent for flipping jazzy samples from the onset, take a listen to the trio's 1997 debut *Fan-Tas-Tic Vol. 1*, specifically the smooth, melancholic tracks "Forth and Back" and "The Look of Love." From the beginning, we can hear how his production was marked by a uniquely off-kilter sense of rhythm that kept listeners on the edge of their seat. Jay Dee would continue to innovate on this drunken style of groove and his disorienting beats lost in time would become his staple, defining his influence and legacy.

When he was eighteen, James would link up with Detroit musician Amp Fiddler — who had played in Funkadelic — who bestowed wisdom on the aspiring musician. Famously, Fiddler would introduce James to his signature piece of music technology and instrument of choice — the Akai

MPC sampler. Equally important, through Fiddler, Jay Dee would meet A Tribe Called Quest's Q-Tip, to whom Jay would hand a Slum Village demo cassette. The tape impressed Q — one of the foremost rappers of all time — prompting the start of a working relationship between Jay Dee and Tribe. Jay Dee was now producing records — under the alias the Ummah — for the Pharcyde, like "Bullshit" and "Runnin'," as well as several cuts on Tribe's 1996 LP *Beats, Rhymes and Life* and 1998's *The Love Movement*. If anything, it was Dilla's strange sense of rhythmic time that attracted Q-Tip, who correctly saw Dilla's beat timing as something unprecedented. His sense of Detroit time out of joint would also be the thing that made Dilla such a universal influence on music of the day.

Next, Jay would also form part of the Soulquarians, a cutting-edge production crew composed of the most iconic musicians of the moment. The members of the all-star lineup included: Questlove, D'Angelo, Erykah Badu, Mos Def, Common, Bilal, Talib Kweli, Q-Tip, Roy Hargrove, James Poyser, and Pino Palladino. Recording at Electric Lady — a studio which shares a spiritual kinship with Detroit since Stevie Wonder recorded there too — the jam sessions would produce some of the most creative music in American popular culture in years. As a member of the Soulquarians, Dilla's influence can be heard on groundbreaking records like the Roots' *Things Fall Apart*, Mos Def's *Black on Both Sides*, Q-Tip's *Amplified*, D'Angelo's *Voodoo*, Erykah Badu's *Mama's Gun*, and Common's *Like Water for Chocolate*. Additionally, Jay's Slum Village would get the Soulquarian treatment for their painfully underappreciated *Fan-Tas-Tic Vol. 2*.

Before passing away from a combination of the rare blood-disease TTP and lupus, J Dilla created sections of his mythologized magnum opus *Donuts* from the hospital. Meticulously crafted with a great deal of intention and precision, J was fully aware the forthcoming record would be his last. In many ways, it is the culmination of Yancey's three decades on this Earth, spent steeped in and studying music. Featuring hundreds of samples, *Donuts* reflects Dilla's crate-digging expertise. The resulting record sounds like a true celebration of life, or perhaps Yancey's musical life flashing before his eyes.

Indeed, *Donuts* is a kaleidoscopic journey through (un) popular music history, featuring the sounds of a lifetime of listening: grainy soul records, dusty breakbeats, forgotten MC's rambling into the mic, television shows, and the ambient sounds of partiers socializing. We hear beloved artists like Kool & the Gang, the Temptations, the Beastie Boys, Frank Zappa, and Dionne Warwick. The website *whosampled.com* has identified 2052 samples associated with Dilla across his production career. This includes both the amount of samples he used and the number of samples attributed to him. If time is a central theme of this chapter, then we might note that *Donuts*' genius lies in its ability to evoke a sense of musical space-time travel, bouncing us from the glory days of Detroit's late Sixties Motown to the Bronx's street corners where neighborhood residents congregated to witness hip-hop MC's birth rap music in real time. When the dust settles, the record comes to thirty-one beats, in line with Dilla's thirty-one years of life. *Donuts* was released on James Yancey's thirty-second birthday, and — just like David Bowie with *Blackstar* — he would pass away a mere three days later.

Dilla's beats and the musical Dilla Time he conjured might be described as "wonky." It's thus no coincidence that musicians making wonky — the largely British sub-genre of music characterized by unquantized beats — consistently cite Dilla as a formative influence. Sitting on the edge of the wonky sub-genre is Burial, the spectral artist that Mark Fisher was most outspoken about championing. There are a host of others, including the Scottish musician Rustie, who would later — in a somewhat typical return of the legacy of Detroit — work with Detroit's other great hip-hop innovator Danny Brown on his 2014 album *Old*.

Wonky achieved its drunken, pleasurably disorienting pull from *going off grid* and employing non-quantized beats. Simply put, quantization is the tool that allows producers to perfectly lock their patterns into place, removing the distinctly human touch of a real player. Dilla foregoes quantization, opting to imbue production with a human element. But if that's all he were doing, his style would be easily replicable and lacking influence. Rather, a closer inspection of Dilla's beat-making reveals a deliberate musical sabotage, where beats are precisely placed in unexpected locations. In this sense, the timings within Dilla's music are an ingenious fusion of machine-like absence and presence.

As noted in *Dilla Time*:

> If the "J Dilla feel" could be achieved simply by turning off timing correct, it stands to reason that another producer might have arrived at that feel long before James Yancey. Nobody did. The innovations of James Yancey bear the mark of a programmer, not a drummer. The sheer *regularity* with which elements like the rushed snare appear is not the result of error or reflex. It is the unmistakable product of his particular use — or misuse, if you prefer — of the MPC.

Sifting Through the Stacks

Of course, the spirit of crate-digging and repurposing the past isn't unique to hip-hop, as the quote from Mick Collins that opens the previous section on Dilla makes clear. Formed initially as a side project to record new types of songs, Collins started one of his many, and currently longest-running alternate projects, the Dirtbombs, in 1995. The concept of this new band was to take old soul and funk tunes and turbo-charge them with the ramshackle rock 'n roll formula that Collins had developed the blueprint for. Their 2001 record *Ultraglide in Black* is a Detroit classic. Composed entirely of covers — with the exception of track four, "Your Love Belongs Under the Rock" — the record reflects the spirit of sifting through the stacks central to this musical moment. Collins' Detroit pride is reflected in covers like "Living for the City," from Stevie Wonder's fantastic 1973 record *Innervisions*. On the Dirtbombs' 2011 record *Party Store*, Collins would further showcase his Detroit pride by releasing a record of garage rock covers of Detroit techno tunes. *Party Store* includes rocking versions of Cybotron's "Alleys of Your Mind," A Number of Names' "Shari Vari," and Inner City's "Good Life." Like Dilla, whose eclectic sampling took in everything, including obscure gems from the progressive rock of the UK's Canterbury scene, Collins further revealed his partiality for the arty, Europhile and avant-garde with a blistering cover of Brian Eno's "King's Lead Hat," a trajectory which would be continued, as we'll see, by Danny Brown in the decades to come.

As a quick aside, we should also acknowledge and pay tribute to the Detroit Cobras, a collectivist garage rock band who've made a career out of revamping forgotten soul, funk, and garage oldies. Like *Ultraglide in Black*, their records are largely comprised of retro tracks given a second (un)life. The result is some of the most fun music you're bound to ever hear. For proof, listen to the opening one-two of "Cha-Cha Twist" and "I'll Keep Holding On" off of their 1998 debut, *Mink, Rat or Rabbit*. The band were known for their revolving door of members, with the only constants over their nearly three-decade career being its co-founders, vocalist Rachel Nagy and guitarist Mary Ramirez. As a result, the group certainly reflects a participatory, community-driven approach to what a band could be.

While this book was being written, in January of 2022, the Detroit Cobras' Rachel Nagy passed away. Once again, I'd like to use the space granted me here to pay my respects to a Detroit garage legend who carried the city's rich legacy of soul, rock, and punk all around the world. Her passionate vocals and knack for injecting forgotten 45s with visceral second life are unmatched. Perhaps her greatest strength was pulling together so many passionate musicians into her orbit, creating both a local and international sense of garage rocker solidarity.

Collins and Nagy, and a hundred others present and past, kept the Detroit garage flame alive and burning bright in the underground, but the band that took it overground on a massive scale is, of course, the White Stripes.

The White Stripes and the Style

I'm too young to have seen the White Stripes live, but when I went to see Jack White at a second sold-out Masonic Temple show in 2022, his commitment to the city was evident in the support act, youthful Detroit garage rockers Sugar Tradition, who were ripping it up as I arrived. It was amazing to see a group of familiar faces that I had seen play around town at empty dive bars and in sweaty basements now in this grandiose space, now performing for a massive crowd of Detroiters. When the trio finished their set, they were met with a thunderous applause. Many around me were gob-smacked at how good they were, and a bunch of people were asking their friends if they knew who the band are. Unsuccessfully trying not to eavesdrop, I butted in and told them. "Are they local?" They most certainly are.

After that, Detroiter Olivia Jean — who had gotten married to White the night prior on-stage — played a rip-roaring set showcasing her signature "garage-goth" sound. Finally, Jack took to the stage for a marathon set of twenty-five career-spanning songs. Yet, the highlight of the night was that earlier moment, championing the local band of twenty-somethings that left the crowd thunderstruck, reminding them that Detroit will always produce something electrifying. But let us return to an earlier moment in time, when the White Stripes themselves were just such a band, still an underdog conquering the world.

Two important sites of garage rock creative exchange were the Gold Dollar and the Old Miami, Detroit's equivalent to New York City's legendary CBGBs and Mudd clubs, located in Midtown's Cass Corridor. While the Gold Dollar is no longer, the Old Miami — a club that was set up by Vietnam veterans — is still a hub for live music. Back in the late Nineties, a new duo who were quickly turning heads began performing alongside other bands from Detroit's garage and punk scene, like the Dirtbombs and the Von Bondies. Composed of two emaciated, ghostly, red-and-white color-coordinated siblings named Jack and Meg, they were called the White Stripes. Sonically, the group cleanly conformed to their scene, with Jack's massive, fuzzy guitar riffs. But with his gift for crafting original earworms, they also stood out amongst their peers. Additionally, a constructed sibling narrative added to a sense of the gothic, but all of the sheen and storytelling wasn't without purpose, and if anything, points to calculated subversion; by taking emphasis off of the fact that the White Stripes were a band playing black blues riffs, they were able to sidestep charges of unoriginality.

The Stripes were unlike trad garage rockers and more in keeping with self-confessed mods like the Gories, who were known for kitting themselves out in suits and shades. Looking like ghosts out of Andy Warhol's New York Factory, Jack and Meg White embodied a certain art-house cool with their pop-modernist aesthetic of strictly red-and-white clothing and instruments. Much of their aesthetic borrowed from and paid homage to the art movement De Stijl, after which they named an album, famed for its irregularly spaced colored grids. It's interesting to note how the beat grids presented by Charnas in *Dilla Time*, which map J Dilla's unconventional time structures, also produces patterns extraordinarily similar to the works produced by Mondrian and others in the De Stijl movement — and as Chalmas insightfully notes, they bear a resemblance to Detroit's own layout of highways and byways, an irregular grid bent and broken by the contours of the older city beneath.

Giving the duo an additional stamp of originality is drummer Meg White's idiosyncratic style and approach. Descending from a lineage that began with the Velvet Underground's Moe Tucker and continued with the Gories' Peggy O'Neill, Meg's style was distinctly manic, a purposefully unconventional way of playing that many in the mainstream failed to understand. There is also an obvious overlap between this lineage and the similarly "drunken" rhythms of J Dilla. Despite working in totally different musical currents, we can see how a particular moment in Detroit history produced musicians thinking and working along similar lines, and there is something between these two artists that speaks of Detroit's simultaneous griddedness and looseness, its incomplete but assertive modernity existing alongside deeper currents of the past that we have found in the work of artists in earlier chapters.

Those familiar with Jack White's ethos and projects know the band was highly conceptualized, and his knowledge of and reverence for music history runs as deep as Dilla's. When the White Stripes' popularity exploded with the release of their 2001 record *White Blood Cells*, they would take their place on the throne of millennial indie rock alongside the Strokes. However, the two bands couldn't be more different.

While the Strokes were emblems of nonchalant, effortless cool, coming up surrounded by the ultra-hip world of New York City's elite music industry connections and nightlife, the White Stripes were an awkward and twitchy duo from a city where no one ever plans to become a star. Further, while the Strokes came from wealthy, well-connected parents that provided them with the ability to travel off to international boarding schools, Jack White was the youngest of ten children, and spent his days obsessively listening to the decidedly uncool records of 1960s blues masters Son House and Blind Willie McTell. Perhaps Jack's ascendency was fated, like blues legends who have an occult mythology — Robert Johnson allegedly sold his soul to the devil at the crossroads — Jack White just so happens to be his mother's Seventh Son, something he alludes to on the Stripes' "Ball and Biscuit."

With *White Blood Cells* containing radio-ready hits like "Fell in Love With a Girl" and the sweet acoustic ballad "We're Going to Be Friends," the duo were on their way to the big time. But it wasn't until 2003, with the release of their LP *Elephant*, that they gave the world the song that would immortalize the band in the halls of music legend: "Seven Nation Army." You've probably heard its pronounced bassline chanted by hyped-up masses of spectators at every single spectacular sports game you've ever attended, and for good reason. An apocalyptic arena anthem to end all arena anthems, "Seven Nation Army" courses with an irrepressible energy in its barebones verses before erupting into a slide guitar riff so catchy that it alone works as the song's hook. It's an absolutely electrifying song, and it's all the more astonishing that it came from a Detroit band who — just two years earlier — had said they had no expectation of becoming successful. But what does "Seven Nation Army", this great stadium anthem of the twenty-first century, soundtrack according to its author? Finishing a performance at his old high school — Detroit's Cass Tech — for a 2019 Bernie Sanders rally with the song, it is clearly the sound of socialism rising in America, just as the riff became the basis for the chant of "Oh-Jeremy-Corbyn" during the Labour leadership campaigns and election cycles that so mystified and infuriated pundits across the Atlantic in the UK in 2017.

In the White Stripes, the band's ethos was one of revamping sounds from the past, but now in his solo career White's philosophy is one of the future. This claim may induce skepticism in those who see White as an analog-obsessed luddite who has a reputation of not owning a cellphone or allowing mobile devices at his shows. Yet, on his latest release, 2022's *Fear of the Dawn*, White embraces a high-tech sonic palette, crystal clear digital mixing and genre-bending experiments. Indeed, at the time of writing, White's most recent direction reads as a garage rock purist who — like a mad, blue-haired scientist — has taken to the laboratory to alchemically craft a record of gut-busting riffs infused with zany studio effects, glitchy manipulations, and detours. In the end, the result is a genuinely unsettling romp through rock 'n roll's potentially carnivalesque future. Moreover, White's ability to pull from the ghosts of music past while experimenting with new sounds and studio techniques has resulted in a discography riddled with pop songs from another dimension, like "My Doorbell" and "Icky Thump," which White humorously reappropriated as "Icky Trump" for a run of T-shirts during the 2016 election cycle.

In the White Stripes' meteoric, stadium rock rise, Jack White would also use the capital he had accumulated to start a record label: Third Man Records. Based initially in Nashville, White would also set up a shop and vinyl pressing plant in Detroit's Midtown Cass Corridor quarter, the same neighborhood where he and Meg once tore up the now-demolished Gold Dollar club. At the time, opening the plant was seen as a big move, since large cultural producers had long moved out of the city. Additionally, White would make good on the promise of not forgetting the scene he started in, signing and reissuing records from Detroit bands like Detroit Cobras, L-Seven, Laughing Hyenas, the Gories, TYVEK, Timmy's Organism, and the Stools. In a move to prevent the erasure of historical records, White would also firmly plant his foot in reissuing out-of-print blues vinyl, marking a push to preserve local music. For example, we can look to the release of thought-to-be-lost recordings from local Tejano pioneer Martin Solis & Los Primos. The record's release was a particularly personal statement, as Solis was a beloved figure in Jack's neighborhood growing up. Few artists of White's wealth, fame and stature have remained so fervently embedded in and committed to the local, to the unvanquished spirit of the Motor City.

I hope what's becoming clear is a uniquely Detroit theme: inhabiting a city overflowing with time, which — like the Great Lakes that surround it — is filled with deep pools, tributaries, and streams of varying depth and intensity. In the 1990s, forgotten music from the past rushes in to collide with the arrested future: underground soul singers of the 1960s could have never imagined their records being beamed back three decades later, souped up with wicked guitar distortion or pitched and stitched together with wonky, Frankensteined breakbeats. Ultimately, the two artistic currents we've traced across this book — guitar-oriented punk and black psychedelia — reconverge in the twenty-first century with a musician who embodies Detroit by pulling something from every one of the city's musical moments and forging something new. Raised on Motown and techno, he adds the next story to the city's towering legacy of black psychedelic music. As a young man, he directly drew inspiration from the White Stripes. Throughout his life, as a crate-digger and committed collectivist, he reminds us of J Dilla's work and the revolving door of musicians that backed the Detroit Cobras. Like Iggy Pop, he is a split subject who oscillates between the death-drive and the assertion of the self-sufficient survivor. In this upcoming stop of our tour through Detroit space-time, we will look at the renaissance man that is Danny Brown.

7. WHEN IT RAIN: ACID RAP AND POST-CAPITALIST DESIRES

All the dead wood from jungles and cities on fire
Can't replace or relate, can't release or repair
Joy Division, "The Atrocity Exhibition"

Got it from Motown
Feel David Ruffin pain
Wanna cry right now
So I'm wishing that it rain
Danny Brown, "Hell for It"

In 2001, a nineteen-year-old Detroiter named Daniel Sewell was — as usual — looking to pick up some girls and catch some bands at his neighborhood's dive bar, the Gold Dollar. Though the club featuring local music was nothing out of the ordinary, Sewell noticed that everyone was treating the band like celebrities. Naturally, Sewell was skeptical of the hype — what made this local rock band special? The vampiric, red-and-white color-coordinated duo took to the stage and launched into a straightforward, blues-punk assault on the crowd's ears. At first, Sewell was unmoved, but when they played a song from their forthcoming album called "Hotel Yorba," everything clicked, and he fell in love with the duo going by the name the White Stripes. Reflecting on the experience in a *Pitchfork* interview, he said:

It changed my life in that sense of knowing that I seen these guys play in a dive bar in Detroit and now they are on MTV and they was winning Grammys after that. They really gave me that inspiration that I could do it on my own terms.

As a child, it is said that, before he could speak, he would babble in rhyme. His mother would read him Dr. Seuss, whose surrealist rhyming books would remain an influence throughout his life. "I'm still influenced by it... *Green Eggs and Ham*? That's my shit." Moreover, as a kid, Sewell was imbibing a diverse and vast swath of musical sounds and styles thanks to his parents' taste. Sewell's father — an amateur DJ — was into Detroit techno and house. Specifically, his father was interested in a high-speed electronic music that fused Chicago house with Detroit's electro and techno at tempos between 145 and 160 BPM. This meant lots of exposure to the futuristic sounds of Juan Atkins and his Cybotron records. Sewell recalls coming home from school and the music from the basement sounding like a fashion show. With these early influences, it's no surprise that Sewell's eventual approach to hip-hop production was just as much J Dilla as it was Dopplereffekt or E-Dancer. Sewell's father also introduced his son to the smooth sounds of the jazz vibraphonist Roy Ayers, as well as the streetwise rap of LL Cool J and A Tribe Called Quest, a group who are instrumental in the life and legacy of J Dilla. His mother was into classic soul and R&B from Motown groups like the Temptations, the Supremes, Four Tops, and more.

Growing up in one of Detroit's toughest neighborhoods, Sewell's predilection for quintessential emblems of nerd culture, like action figures and video games, made him something of an alienated kid. But he also had an undeniable charm, a certain confidence and coolness that came straight from Wu-Tang Clan's *Enter the 36 Chambers*, a CD the young Sewell listened to on a loop. Indeed, Wu-Tang were the template for Brown, who admired them for being authentically hood and simultaneously unabashed geeks, something evidenced by RZA's repeated sampling of obscure and, at that time, hard-to-find old-school kung-fu films. Between the Temptations, A Tribe Called Quest, and Wu-Tang Clan, it's possible to believe that the power of black collectivity in music-making was — at least subconsciously — embedded in Daniel's psyche, and these influences would later resurface in the form of his own collective, Bruiser Brigade.

When he turned to drug dealing, Sewell landed himself in jail, an event that convinced him to double down on his burgeoning artistic endeavors and strengthened his belief in redemption. Upon his release, the resilient young man emerged anew as Danny Brown and began releasing his *Detroit State of Mind* series of mixtapes. He would befriend Tony Yayo of 50 Cent's G-Unit, and the pair would release their collaborative record *Hawaiian Snow*. Due to the association, many speculated that Brown would sign with 50 Cent, but unwilling to compromise on his Detroit image of fitted jeans and punk rock aesthetics, he ultimately did not fit with the label. Further frustrated with the industry's partiality for 50 Cent-inspired beats, Brown returned to the sound of Detroit, and that was, of course, J Dilla.

With the release of his debut record, 2010's kaleidoscopic *The Hybrid*, Brown succeeded in turning every eye in the hip-hop industry toward him. Featuring a slew of forward-thinking beats that found him rapping with passionate swagger, *The Hybrid* showcased Brown as a wholly original talent. Some of the record's otherworldly production is credited to Detroit's own Quelle Chris, who has gone on to have his own successful career as a rapper. Out of the gates, Brown stakes his claim to the throne on "Greatest Rapper Ever," before paying homage to dance music with the pulsing, rave-inflected "Need Another Drink." Perhaps most significantly on "White Stripes," Brown pays tribute to the band who inspired him over a thumping garage rock beat, re-asserting the ways in which soul and garage, punk, rock, and rap are all uniquely intertwined parts of Detroit's musical DNA. The record was rightfully championed as one of the great tapes of the year, and had underground hip-hop heads from across the country hanging on whatever Danny would drop next. That next release — Brown's explosive sophomore record — would solidify him as the most idiosyncratic new voice in rap.

Showcasing a completely uncategorizable sound that contrasted lit party bangers with hazy, drug-fueled dirges on 2012's *XXX*, Brown garnered critical acclaim and a cult following. Supplementing his music with a larger-than-life persona, he stepped into the limelight as a hero for outcasts, the Adderall Admiral. The album's title is a witty triple-entendre: three X's to signify the Roman numeral 30, a reference to the age Brown was at time of recording; a hint at the pornographic material inside the record sleeve; and a reference to the ecstasy, then known as X, that had begun to seep into hip-hop culture from EDM, changing the sonic palette, shifting the tempos and adding a new hedonic-depressive dynamic to the music. The highlights of the record were a slew of off-kilter party bangers like "Die Like a Rockstar" and "Monopoly." While Brown displayed a more thoughtful side on melancholic tracks like the comedown cut "Party All the Time," he also offered up a sobering reflection on cyclical, generational addiction with "DNA." Ultimately, *XXX* garnered critical acclaim and massive hype, putting considerable pressure on Brown to produce an equally game-changing follow-up.

In 2013, he emerged with his cult-classic *Old*, an album which found Brown oscillating between euphoric bliss and soul-crushing lows, rapping confessional over old-school beats on side-A and turning up to hyper EDM-trap drops on side-B. Similar to Ian Curtis — a spectral figure who has stalked the pages of this book and who perhaps began to stalk Brown around this time too — the album reflects a destructive bipolarity. Mirroring the mountainous highs and ocean-floor lows of Brown's work, Joy Division guitarist Bernard Sumner noted that "Ian was into the extremities of life." Joy Division's song "Digital" is instructive here. As Kevin Cummins notes:

> The lyrics of "Digital" are actually digital. There's on, off, day in, day out, day in, day out. And they're switching. It's also somehow weirdly related to Curtis' persona itself, which, we know now, is bipolar.

Similarly, Danny Brown embodies his generation's digital hyper-saturation with a twitchy and glitched-out entanglement in the communicative matrices that rule over us. The "day in, day out" here is the remorseless routine of building a brand, trying to stay ahead of the trends and maintaining an online persona in the "attention economy." Brown has an always switched-on, plugged-in online presence, broadcasting thoughts in real time on the panic-inducing hellscape of Twitter, conducting gaming streams on Twitch, and now has his own talk program, *The Danny Brown Show*. Social media is a way of constructing another self. It is a vehicle for creating artistic characters, unleashing alternate personas, and revealing late-night diaristic confessions. From the beginning, Brown used this entity-making machine to lean into a lovable clown character that was simultaneously hurting, struggling to cope. At a certain point, the character could eclipse the man. This is Baudrillard's notion of hyperreality, a world where the simulations that proliferate are more real than reality itself. Trapped in the hyperreal, Brown's psychedelia recreates the feeling of soft narcosis: blitzed and burnt out on the dopamine rush of Twitter notifications, a never-ending timeline of fifteen-second TikToks, and lonely, late-night Tinder swiping.

The danger, of course, is that the online performance and the persona eclipses the person themselves, becoming their master, an alienated uncanny double whose endless demands their creator ends up in thrall to. As many of us know, cyberspace's eerie pull makes demands on us: keep the persona alive, participate more, satisfy the algorithm. It's that or watch one's digital corpse fade away. No one can play the game forever, and for anyone invested in keeping their uncanny double maintained, a rupture is bound to occur. Brown would chronicle that incoming collision, his psychic crash, on his next record.

Acid Rap

Before we look at that epochal work, we ought to note that Brown's style of rap descends from a uniquely Detroit heritage. In some ways, his success represents this particular rap lineage finally emerging from the underground, albeit in a somewhat mutated and X-irradiated form. Back in the late 1980s, as Brannon and the whole host of hardcore kids were battling with their demons, a Detroit teenager named Esham would pioneer the rap subgenre known as "horrorcore" in order to deal with his own demons. Recorded when he was just sixteen years old, Esham's 1989 release *Boomin' Words from Hell* was a trailblazing work that reflected the small Detroit rap scene's partiality for the gothic, the obscene, and over-the-top violence. Esham explores themes of paranoia, suicide, violence, and drugs in order to paint a cartoonish hellscape vision of Detroit deprivation, and his continued influence on the lyrical preoccupations of Detroit hip-hop artists cannot be understated, observable in everyone ranging from the Insane Clown Posse to the city's most notorious son,

Eminem, whose obscene lyricism clearly descends from Detroit horrorcore.

Marshall Mathers — or Eminem — is one the most famous and acclaimed rappers to come out of Detroit, and it might not be going too far to claim that he is also one of the most famous musical artists of all time. Unfortunately, though, Em's success has gone so far that he often eclipses his city's other creative achievers, with the story of Detroit hip-hop often beginning and ending with him. The Real Slim Shady had arrived before he officially began. His debut record, *The Slim Shady LP*, would go on to sell platinum several times over and Mathers would star in his own semi-autobiographical film, *8 Mile*. The movie — a classic underdog rise-to-fame affair — depicts Detroit legendary venue the Shelter, where Em delivers one of the most iconic moments of any music film: a crowd-unifying battle-rap-winning verse. Over Mobb Deep's "Shook Ones" beat, Em in the final battle gets the whole club's hands up with the immortal words, "Everybody in the 313, put your hands up and follow me." Did it really happen? Can we ever know for sure? Though we're left to speculate, it's undeniably dope to watch Em's star power kick in, the moment where he knows he's won the people over, at least for the time being.

If Eminem is a revered, central figure in recent hip-hop, Insane Clown Posse are a more marginal and often derided group. Nonetheless, it's Insane Clown Posse who best exemplify the Detroit spirit in all its solidarity, fierce localism, determined independence, and gothic yearning for the weird. At the time of *XXX*'s release, Brown aligned himself with the Juggalos, performing at their 13th Gathering. For the uninitiated, the Juggalos is the name for the subcultural fan group that follow Detroit hip-hop duo Insane Clown Posse, who have formed their own intensely loyal, fringe, subcultural community, revolving around clown makeup and drinking the Michigan-made pop Faygo. Immensely important to Juggalos' sense of community is their annual gathering, a self-organized festival to which their cultishly devoted fanbase travels from across the land to convene.

Insane Clown Posse and the Juggalos' grotesque aesthetic, repulsive to most, are one of the key reasons for their enormous but almost invisible success. Without radio play or TV exposure, even back in the pre-internet days they were able to build up a considerable following and launch their own, highly successful label Psychopath Records. Ever since, Insane Clown Posse have managed to be truly independent. For the fans, they exist as a reserve of the non-coopted within the cycle of the continuous appropriation of emerging artists and trends by record labels and big business. If capital constantly thwarts our attempts to forge scenes, collectives, and new expressions of our own by turning them into marketable commodities, Insane Clown Posse have represented a wellspring of something beyond or above mere product, and so, for their devotees — for all their obsession with the grisly and the abject — the group have remained something the Juggalos deeply identify as being their own. This sense of an outsider community, in which everyone is bonded by their passion for staying independent and underground, means the Faygo-spraying Juggalos have a much deeper commitment to solidarity and mutual aid than most explicitly leftist organizations, and it would thus make sense that Danny Brown felt fit to perform at the gathering. As we'll see, Brown's philosophy is one of community too.

Curiously, though, Esham, the originator of horrorcore, actually prefers to describe his sound as "acid rap," because the dark, hallucinatory dreamscapes he conjures up resemble the wall-melting visions that an LSD trip might produce. Ultimately, if Brown descends from and extends a Detroit lineage, combining Esham's hallucinatory acid rap with trippy techno, then it makes sense to suggest that, perhaps, rather than acid rap, Brown's thrillingly disorienting time-, space-, genre-, and persona-twisting trips might best be characterized as a form of very twenty-first-century, post-Web 2.0. digital black psychedelia.

This is the Way, Step Inside

INTERVIEWER: What kind of kid were you? Were you outgoing? Shy?

DANNY BROWN: I think I was just goofy. [...] I was never cool, you know what I'm saying? I was just goofy.

I can't sleep my anxiety is at an all time high but don't none of y'all care about that shit ... Y'all just want me to be goofy.
@xdannyxbrownx, Twitter Feb. 10th, 2014

On 13th June 2016, Danny Brown posted a distorted photo of himself with the cryptic caption "#WhenItRain." As it would turn out, the *Videodrome*-esque post was hinting at the first single of a forthcoming album. Accompanied with a color-saturated VHS music video, "When It Rain" finds Brown tripping on distorted, digital nostalgia. Aesthetically, it may also be pulling from Outkast's similarly color-saturated music video for "B.O.B.," which Brown would sample a line from later in the album on the cut, "Today." The single's artwork features Brown sprawled out on purple grass, blissed out in some sort of hallucinogenic trip, again hinting at the theme of psychedelia the upcoming project seemed to be embracing. The track itself provides us with an updated commentary on Detroit, linking the trip on the single's artwork to his environment:

Know it's fucked up, that's how it be

Growing up living every day in the D
And it don't seem like shit gon' change
No time soon in the City of Boom
Doomed from the time we emerged from the womb
So to cope, drugs we consume

Yet "When It Rain" was foreshadowing something bigger to come.

I received *Atrocity Exhibition* on vinyl in a record swap with a friend, and I eagerly rushed home to play it. I was perplexed, roused, and, from then on, obsessed with the obscene piece of art I had been given. If 2013's *Old* was characterized by a bipolar display of Brown's two symbolic sides, then *Atrocity Exhibition* is the mask slipping, revealing the real. The album cover sees Danny glitched out, rendered through the lens of a hazy VHS filter, revealing that half of his face is a metallic-looking skull. If before Brown had two faces, two modes of engagement, and oscillated between them, the death-driven Danny and the Party Danny, here they are linked together in the same person on a single visual plane. In the horizontal black lines striking through the title, we see the trace of Joy Division's *Unknown Pleasures* rippling beneath the technicolor too, revealing yet another connection between Brown and the darkest corners of post-punk. If across music space-time we've observed a portal between Joy Division's Manchester and the musicians of Acid Detroit, Brown's fourth album makes that connection explicitly clear, with the title taken from the opening track of Joy Division's 1980 suicide-foreshadowing record *Closer*, which Joy Division themselves took from J.G. Ballard's experimental novel of distorted vignettes.

Post-punk, goth, and industrial are the record's touchstones. Indeed, Brown stated he was also inspired by Talking Heads, and he wanted to create the hip-hop equivalent of Nine Inch Nails' *Downward Spiral*, an album famous for its portrayal of mental illness. Going further, the record's $70,000 worth of psychedelic samples digitizes and reconfigures forgotten or eerily familiar sounds — faintly recognizable, distant but not identifiable, now warped as if trapped in a fun-house hall of mirrors. The album's influences, from the title on, represent a further stage in the cycling back and forth of inspiration between the UK and the US, Detroit and Manchester, Iggy and the Bellville Three's Europhilia and fascination with Krautrock, alongside Joy Division. One of the standout tracks, the single "Pneumonia," was produced by the British artist Evian Christ, whose biography perfectly reveals the extent to which futurist ideas and connections proliferate back and forth. Christ, whose real name is Joshua Leary, began his artistic journey playing on the old keyboards his father used to make music inspired by Kraftwerk with, making J-Dilla influenced soul beats, and then diving into the techno dominated world of DJing. Thus, on *Atrocity Exhibition*, the music of Detroit returns in a mutated form, filtered through the lens of outsiders.

Opening with the track "Downward Spiral" — which echoes *XXX*'s opening cut, as well as Nine Inch Nails' 1994 record of the same name — it is immediately evident that *Atrocity Exhibition* is Brown's full-on descent into paranoia, the brutal reality of excessive sex, partying, raving, drugs, and other destructive vices. One of *Atrocity Exhibition*'s core themes is substance abuse as a means of coping with overwhelming circumstances. The record is filled with allusions to drug addiction, which Brown is no stranger to. However, the power of *Atrocity Exhibition* isn't in the way that Brown raps about drugs, but rather the way that his music replicates the feeling of being *on* drugs. But rather than indulging in the standard pleasures of party rap, Brown's drug of choice — like all ravers — is E.

Ecstasy, a drug that gained popularity at acid house

raves in the 1980s, is unique in that it delivers both the perception-altering effects of acid and heartbeat-raising highs of stimulants. Paired with body-rattling bass and beats, MDMA — or Molly, as American users will know it — is thus a natural choice for the rave-inflected acid rap of Danny Brown. Like a psychedelic speed, Molly encourages feelings of friendship and euphoria, which seem to match-up with Brown's blissed-out demeanor.

Take the first lyrics of the record for evidence:

I'm sweating like I'm in a rave
Been in this room for three days
Think I'm hearing voices
Paranoid think I'm seeing ghosts-es

Indeed, *Atrocity Exhibition* is the traumatic eruption of what Jacques Lacan called "the Real" — Brown, aging and strung out, hitting the limits of what his body and mind can contain and process, is confronted with his own materiality, the possibility of collapse and death. Rather than a drug-numbed and disembodied Internet avatar, he is in fact suffering flesh and blood. There is a physical substrate that is slowly being poisoned, going wrong, a skull beneath his skin. But it's still unclear what he can do, other than sit back and watch, or perhaps worse still, simply push it further for the abject thrill of watching himself come apart. Here it's perhaps not the time but rather the self that is out of joint. "I think that each performance [Ian Curtis] gave that I saw was the real deal, the raw truth." Brown, like Brannon and Ian Curtis, seems to have concluded that the ultimate truth at the core of life is one of depression. As Fisher elaborates in *Ghosts of My Life*:

That is why Joy Division can be a very dangerous drug for young men. They seem to be presenting The Truth (they present themselves as doing so). Their subject, after all, is depression. Not sadness or frustration, rock's standard downer states, but depression: depression, whose difference from mere sadness consists in its claim to have uncovered The (final, unvarnished) Truth about life and desire.

On *Atrocity Exhibition*, Brown swims in the icy waters of depression, lamenting on "Downward Spiral" that the bottomless pit of numbness results in a necessity to "isolate myself, don't go nowhere," and that he is "thinking irrational, I have no emotions." While on the second track, "Tell Me What I Don't Know," he regales us with a story of a friend who wanted "new Jordans and some bitches" being shot and killed at the liquor store back when they were just young men. It is this traumatizing exposure to violence that still haunts Brown's psyche, inducing what feels like an unconquerable persistence of paranoia. This theme of bearing witness to and being haunted by footage of violence reveals another meaning of the album, which Brown himself confirmed in an *NPR* interview:

> When they see anything happen... like say police or anything that's violent that's happening, instead of them trying to fix the situation, what do they do? They pull they phone out and try to record it... We living in an atrocity exhibition.

The album's themes of drug burnout and a lost future persist with the track "Rolling Stone." The track makes Brown's connections to digital black psychedelia explicitly clear. Born out of a direct message exchange on Twitter with the song's featuring artist Petite Noir at 4am, "Rolling Stone" reflects how the weird world of late-night scrolling forms a network of similarly lonesome creatives. As cyberspace lends itself to increasingly globalized creative webs, linking people across the world in real-time, we can all become anonymous nomads lost in social media's back alleys, strange side streets, and underground passageways, slowly becoming strangers to ourselves in the ever-shifting miasma of fleeting connections, fragments, and sensation.

The closest thing approaching one of Danny's classic party bangers is the magnetic centerpiece of the album, "Ain't It Funny." This monstrous track points out the absurd and crushing speed in which things can so quickly spiral downwards to a rock-bottom low, leaving nothing but the spectacle of disintegration as entertainment. Ain't it funny how it happens? Ain't it funny how it went from so good to so bad, so quickly? Ain't it funny how no one cares? Ain't it funny how the greatest city in the world is marked by a certain degree of anarchic chaos? Aint it? In this way, Detroit and Brown share something in common — the spectacle of their ruin is mere titillation for those who don't have to live it.

Mark Fisher never commented on the album, but given his interests, it's hard to believe he wouldn't have been both thematically and sonically engaged by a record that came from a cutting-edge hip-hop artist that drew on Ballard, Joy Division, the gothic and post-punk, in order to address addiction and the burnout that comes from too many juiced-up hours on the hedonic treadmill, caught up in the compulsion to pursue pleasure at all costs, enjoyment having become the main meaning and horizon of activity in the neoliberal economy. That Brown seems to eventually get off that treadmill and reorient himself to the world, that he hits rock bottom and, like Brannon — but unlike Curtis — manages to come through it, is something we'll look at next.

Because, for all of the record's darkness, Brown ends *Atrocity Exhibition* with a vision of light at the end of the tunnel. On closing track "Hell for It," Brown lets it be known that, despite the vices that threaten to end his life, he fully intends to live through it, to see the morning light, even if, at each dawn, he dies. He damns his enemies, letting them know the transcendent power of making art has imbued him with the purpose in life needed to persevere through it all. Brown is an artist who's possessed with a love for art and his city, which makes him strong enough to weather the icy storms of both Michigan's winters and the depressed mind. It's this love that is essential to Detroit's ethos. We love it here, and we love it because we love each other.

Old Dawn Fades

EVE: *So this is your wilderness. Detroit.*
ADAM: *Everybody left*
EVE: *What's that?*
ADAM: *It's the Packard plant, where they once built the most beautiful cars in the world. Finished.*
EVE: *But this place will rise again.*
ADAM: *Will it?*
EVE: *Yeah. There's water here. And when the cities in the South are burning, this place will bloom.*

Only Lovers Left Alive

If Brown's music on *Atrocity Exhibition* is acid rap, then it's acid as a painful, caustic dissolvent of the self, rather than a freeing of the ego into a crystalline, oneiric realm. Brown's predilection for drugs — like the increased prevalence of drugs in hip-hop culture, from weed via Cypress Hill, Snoop Dog, and *The Chronic* in the Nineties to the Molly that dominated the 2000s, on to percs, lean and a polydrug arsenal of over-the-counter and unregulated pharmaceuticals — reveals that, even on his party album *XXX*, the downside was already evident. It's on *Atrocity* where the psychological and neurological burnout, as well as the physical symptoms, become overwhelming. Yet, for many, the first step to moving past trauma is confronting it in a painful process of naming the symptoms and events. By purging his psyche of the violence he's both witnessed and inflicted, he sets himself up to break on through to the other side, residing in a healing state of mind.

If *Atrocity* is Brown's gothic record, then the film that provides the visual backdrop for the album is certainly Jim Jarmusch's 2013 film *Only Lovers Left Alive*. Fittingly, Jarmusch's foreboding vampiric film follows two vampires, Adam and Eve — played by Tom Hiddleston and Tilda Swinton respectively — who have survived for centuries on blood, preferably supplied by doctors. The vampire couple have been responsible for influencing some of the most famous musicians, artists, and scientists in history, yet they must remain anonymous, their contributions destined to be credited to others.

It is fitting that Hiddleston's Adam — aesthetically reminiscent of Jack White — is a holed-up Detroit musician who records analog-drenched post-rock records, which he anonymously distributes at burned-out punk clubs. Myth proliferates about this mysterious musician who fails to credit his records. Eventually, curious kids turn up at Adam's house to find out who the music's author is. Like the Detroit musicians we have surveyed in this book, the vampires' influence is profound, but the credit is often misattributed to the personas they have inspired and assumed.

In 2019, Brown re-emerged with a change of speed and style. He had been known for his famously unfixed teeth and a distinctive grunge aesthetic that resembled first-wave punk rockers and goths, perhaps even catching associations with the disturbing heroin chic of the 1990s. Now, Brown returned to the public eye with a perfect set of pearly whites and streetwise style. Many fans were proud, happy that

Brown — in erasing the traces of his former self — seemed to be turning a corner for his health. Sonically and lyrically, his new album, *uknowhatimsaying¿*, finds Brown going from buckling under the weight of No Future to living his best life. Just looking at the album cover, we see that Brown has changed from a low-resolution, grainy VHS image, to a lush pastel palette that might evoke tie-dye. Produced by Dilla's long-time collaborator Q-tip, *uknowhatimsaying¿* draws the album back into a certain Detroit heritage. On "Best Life," Q imbues the tune with psychedelic-soul majesty by flipping a sample of "To Make You Happy," a forgotten 1973 soul tune from Michigan singer Tommy McGee. The track's music video is also instructive. Surrounded by hanging floral arrangements and various shots of community, it is here, more than anywhere else, that we see Brown move from digital depression-sufferer to solar soul rapper.

Simultaneously, given Brown's own Anglophilia, the album finds inspiration from the dance genre — not to be confused with the rock stylings of MC5 or the Gories — UK garage. Additionally, Brown yet again enlists UK producer Paul White, who handles production on the album's misty, rave-inflected cuts. For example, on the record's titular track, White seems to pull inspiration from Detroit house legend Moodymann, with a misty, bumping beat. With its blown-out bass and four-on-the-floor kicks, White imbues the tune with all of the joyous energy of a communal kick-back.

In some ways, the passage from *XXX* to *uknowhatimsaying¿* mirrors in microcosm the shift in the UK between ecstatic but anxious rave, darkly Dionysian jungle, and then onto the new dawn of a sensual, celebratory garage. To draw a very simple and obvious illustration of this shift, some of the most famous of jungle tracks draw on films like *Terminator* for their Futurist man-machine hybrid aesthetic and militant, masculinist ethic (and it's also worth noting here the ways in which the cover of *Atrocity Exhibition* mirrors the classic image of Schwarzenegger's Terminator, with its synthetic skin peeled back to reveal the metal exoskeleton beneath). But by the time jungle had morphed into UK garage, the themes of the music had changed dramatically. For example, Sweet Female Attitude's "Flowers", one of the biggest UK garage tracks, is a gentle mingling of sensibilities, shared vulnerabilities and tenderness, and an expression of love and commitment to healing and restoration:

I'll bring you flowers in the pouring rain
Living without you is driving me insane
I'll bring you flowers, I'll make your day
The tears you cry, I'll dry them all away

When Brown asks on "When It Rain", "Ain't no water, how a flower gon' grow?," he is wishing for rain so that, in the barren desert of depression, the flowers can begin to bloom again. But most of all, the movement from the tortured darkness of *Atrocity Exhibition* to the light ethereality of *uknowhatimsaying¿* yet again drives home the point that Detroiters, like Detroit itself, will always adapt and persevere.

If Jarmusch's *Only Lovers Left Alive* captures the gothic, undead Detroit reflected in *Atrocity Exhibition* — and, by extension, the atomized and insatiable, melancholy subjects of late capitalism — then it is Ryan Gosling's 2014 directorial debut, *Lost River*, which best depicts the acid-washed Detroit of *uknowhatimsaying¿*. While Jarmusch's film languishes in desolate, depressed night rides, Gosling's finds the city brimming with weird excesses and potentials for regrowth. And while both films entertain a degree of the magical, *Lost River*'s tone leans into the fantastical and transcendent. The movie is about a city — a thinly veiled Detroit — on the verge of being subsumed, drowned like an Atlantis, by impending flooding. If one aspect of acid communism is the aestheticization of everyday life, then *Lost River* and *uknowhatimsaying¿* provide a glimpse of what a post-capitalist future may look and sound like. For the real magic of *Lost River* lies not so much in its plot, which is riddled with art-house cliches, but rather in Benoit Debie's hazy, neon-lit cinematography. Debie bathes the city in lush hues and grainy textures that hint at burbling growth amidst the ruins, paralleling the encroachment of waves of multi-colored blooms into the collapsing homes and autos of the Detroiters in Brown's "Best Life" video. The opening shots of the film are perhaps most instructive. Bones, one of the film's protagonists, out looking for scrap metal to sell, walks through an overgrowth of tall grass, which brims with a presence, a lifeforce lurking in the dew-covered weeds and marsh.. This is a vision of Detroit in which nature reclaims the city, its denizens repurpose spaces from its industrial past, art adorns the crumbling walls and the urban and rural beautifully coexist.

What *Only Lovers Left Alive* only gives us a glimpse of, *Lost River* makes visually clear. Like its vampire protagonists, *Only Lovers Left Alive* is afraid of the sunlight. Indeed, what the film fails to fully capture is the other side of Detroit's eerie-weird dichotomy: a searing post-capitalist desire that threatens to rupture the old, blood-sucking systems of power. That said, in the following final chapter, let us survey Detroit's most current music scenes, commitments to collectivity, and strategies for leading the country in sustainability.

8. POINTING TO A POST-CAPITALIST DETROIT

The people who live here are mainly the descendants of Africa Americans who came from the South and who through generations and decades of slavery and Jim Crow had become convinced we can make a way out of nowhere. People who had been raised down south and had grown their own food began to look at the vacant lots not s so much as blight but as promise.as a place where you could not only begin growing your own food but also where you could bring about a kind of cultural revolution in the minds of young people who were used to the quick fixes of city life.

Grace Lee Boggs, *We Are Not Ghosts*

In Mark Dworkin and Melissa Young's extraordinary 2011 documentary of urban resilience, *We Are Not Ghosts*, we see how communities strategically combat and push back against the unfulfilled promises of the city's government and negative perceptions that come from the outside. The film's title rings out like an affirmation of the hauntological line of thought we discussed in the techno chapter, as it depicts Detroiters who aren't thinking about bringing back the factories and the Fordism that came with them. On the contrary, the Detroiters of *We Are Not Ghosts* are engaging with the immediate opportunities opened up by the abandonment of capital. Never trapped or confined to the past, Detroiters always look forward to the future. In local rhythms, expressive art sessions and neighborhood solidarity, the documentary showcases just how the city is once again pioneering the way into a better world. Crucially,

We Are Not Ghosts asserts that this is not a haunted ghost town, but a bustling city where real people live real lives. Inviting the specter in, the preoccupation with degradation and "ruin porn" is patronizing and dehumanizing, especially when there are examples of the contrary all around. The city's population may have shrunk, but it's not vacant, and shouldn't be treated as such.

For over a decade, Detroit journalist John Gallagher — author of the books *Reimagining Detroit* and *Revolution Detroit* — has been examining the city's unique, emerging solutions to urban degradation. Though Detroit was marked by the postmodern condition that Francis Fukuyama called "the end of history," Gallagher notes in an interview with *United States of Green* that, "Detroit has a ways to go. We are not recovered, we are recovering. But, the notion that Detroit was at the end of history — it rose and fell — has been completely discredited." Let's take a moment to survey some of the emerging solutions Gallagher has helpfully pointed to.

Taking up the gauntlet, we address the issue of vacant space. One solution Gallagher looks to is community gardening and self-sustainable food projects. Urban farming is the simple idea that taking vacated, polluted land and cleaning it up for the sake of repurposing it as productive is a good thing — and it has taken hold in Detroit. Scattered throughout the city are urban gardens and farms — it's not uncommon to see goats and chickens — which contribute to a burgeoning local food system. The fruits of this labor can be observed when taking a stroll through Eastern Market on a bustling Saturday morning, where local farmers sell fresh food to throngs of Detroiters. It can also be seen in projects like Recovery Park and Earthworks Urban Farm. However, farming is hard work, and it is harder still to find enthusiastic, committed individuals to stick with it, so it is a strategy that will continue to take some time to develop.

Another hopeful change is the return of small, local businesses. For years, Detroit has been associated with major industrial corporatism, but now it seems the tide is turning, as the city is making way for a plethora of smaller-scale ventures. These smaller operation managers have a better sense of the communities they're serving, rather than the cold tentacles of global capital, whose indifference to the local population was palpable. With the Big Three — General Motors, Chrysler and Ford — moving out, Gallagher said in a 2018 interview that "there's been this whole notion that Detroit's now pivoting from gargantuan corporate power structures to a much more nimble entrepreneurial-based economy." Indeed, Detroit has become a nexus for interesting changes, turning itself from the poster child of urban degradation to a leading hub of innovation.

Another promising post-capitalist phenomenon is the proliferation of public space and art installations. One famous example is the Heidelberg Project. Located in the McDougall-Hunt neighborhood on the city's East side, the outdoor art installation was started in 1986 by artist Tyree Guyton, who made the project as a protest and tribute to his childhood neighborhood, which began to disintegrate in the wake of the 1967 rebellion. Though it's been around for a longtime, on its thirtieth anniversary in 2016, Guyton announced that the installation would be systematically dismantled as preparations for a new iteration of the project would begin to take place. Specifically, the Heidelberg Project is to take on a collective, community arts-based approach, which promises to be quite interesting. Another public art installation is Hamtramck Disneyland. A beautiful example of folk art, Hamtramck Disneyland is located right in resident Dmytro Szylak's front yard for all to view. After working for thirty years at Chrysler Motors, Szylak — newly retired and looking for a hobby to pass the time — constructed Hamtramck Disneyland piece by piece over a five-year period between 1992 and 1997. It is in a yellow-and-blue color scheme to reflect Szylak's Ukrainian heritage.

For another interesting, productive repurposing of space, we can look to the Russell Industrial Center. Once an industrial factory, it is now home to the largest arts community in the Midwest. Featuring rooms of various sizes, from small to a whole factory floor, it has become a hub for painters, glassblowers, punk bands, DJs, DIY recording studios, and more. The epic, Albert Kahn-designed seven-building structure also hosts concerts, raves, a monthly local art market, and a marijuana dispensary.

Finally, we might note that — despite George Clinton declaring that we've knocked her up on "Maggot Brain" — Mother Nature is healing in Detroit. Along the banks of the river, for the first time in years, Bald Eagles and other native creatures, like Sturgeons and White Fish, are returning. Meanwhile, though the Detroit river has historically had water too polluted to swim in, these days you can find Detroiter's along the banks on hot summer days, jumping in the water to bathe and splash around.

The importance of all these hopeful signs was brilliantly summed up in the concluding post of a series in the Detroit subreddit on building a tourism strategy. The post's author, founder of Detroit focused blog Fresh Coast Thoughts named Zach Kilgore, eloquently summed it up when he wrote the following in a section of the post entitled "The World Needs Detroit":

In the 40s, the world needed us to save democracy. After the war, the world needed us to build their cars and make their music. Today, the world needs us to show them how we can go through hell and live to tell the tale.

A lot of us have been feeling like we're heading for a dark place. In 2020, the pandemic began. In 2021, half the country was flooded while the other half was on fire. In 2022, we're seeing the clearest signs yet that the America we know is at risk of being lost for good.

Detroit isn't just a city or even an identity — it's a beacon of hope. The world needs us because we are proof that if we focus on what's important, we can overcome the toughest obstacles. Through our determination and dedication, we can weather any storm, and we can enter a new, more just era of prosperity.

That said, this is a story that points to something hopeful. The long, dark road of Detroit history can be seized upon as an enormous opportunity for reinvention, reprioritization, and new thinking.

One of Mark Fisher's favorite works by his long-time musical hero, Ultravox founder John Foxx, revolves around something like the Green Detroit that is beginning to emerge in the areas that have been untouched by gentrification. Curiously, it's perhaps worth noting that Foxx has a track called "Only Lovers Left Alive." The story-album in question is called *The Quiet Man* and it follows a man drifting through a depopulated London that is being reclaimed by nature. A standard trope of many post-apocalyptic fantasies, it is narrated over the sounds of birdsong, pulling the listener into a tranquil state that evokes Detroit's commitment to regenerating without regeneration, to community gardens, art spaces, low-tech and low-impact forms of travel and production, of opening up the city land to other uses, and educating its citizens to alternate currents of thought and traditions that stem from Black diasporic struggles and visions — those same struggles, visons and traditions that brought us Motown and the image of the Psychedelic Shack. Spaces of fellowship and ease, spaces in which the built and the natural, art and self-expression, cultivation and community mesh, and new, numinous aesthetics of everyday life are being born.

As we have seen in the art of many of Detroit's denizens, simply weathering one's darkest night guarantees the searing light of the morning sun rising up, over the chrome skyline. A new day will dawn, and we can emerge from the ashes stronger than before. Out of this steel rubble, we cannot say or guess. For now, we know only a heap of broken images, a fractured history. But these fragments of sound and vision can be reordered, pieced together to reveal lurking potential and reclaimed futures. As Fisher once wrote, "From a situation in which nothing can happen, suddenly anything is possible again." Yes, anything is possible in Detroit, the home of Motown, techno, and punk. With a little bit of psychedelic reason, we can free our minds, build a castle from a grain of sand, and enter the fun house once again. But what will be the soundtrack to the glorious rebirth?

The New Underground

RICH TUPICA: Has playing in a band in Detroit changed over the years?

MICK COLLINS: I get asked that a lot, and it hasn't. The only thing that has changed is the music that influences people and in Detroit, even that hasn't changed much because it's still a lot of the same influences. It's just interpreted differently these days. It's the same and vibrant as it ever was, there is just no one looking right now, that's all. There's no huge media attention, but there is still a million bands and bars and art galleries all across town that will let you play. It's all still there.

As the above exchange with Mick Collins reveals, Detroit's garage rock scene remains a thriving, underground hub of bands expanding upon the music of the city's forebears. New bands are constantly growing out of the city's nourishing pool of young musicians. In keeping with tradition, they remain committed to analog, cassettes, and all things DIY. Young punk bands can be found ripping it up at venues across town, but the contemporary scene can perhaps be said to be headquartered in the historically Polish neighborhood of Hamtramck, with bands often cutting their teeth at the luminous Outer Limits Lounge. Located away from any main streets, but rather right in midst of the neighborhood's houses, Outer Limits is firmly embedded within the residential community. Buzzing with the carnivalesque energy of a bazaar, Outer Limits is a psychedelic shack that finds itself not only on the outer limits of space, but time and consciousness. As the lounge's website attests, if you ever find yourself there, "I'm certain you'll find your visit most illuminating."

Regularly playing alongside dynamite trio the Stools, who we mentioned in Chapter 6, modern scene staples include Toeheads and 208. Toeheads are a trio — Jake Aho, Joey Hanania, and Derek Burbank — with a classic garage sound influenced by Detroit punk and 1960s Nuggets groups. Like all the other bands of this new era, they came up in the house show scene, playing relentlessly and regularly to audiences looking to party, booze, and blow off steam on weekend nights. That said, they're house rock at its absolute best. Meanwhile, 208 — a duo composed of Kyle Edmonds and Shelby Say — play blown-out, degraded garage punk. Taking Phil Spector production to its most extreme, they are known for conjuring massive walls of sound that keep the mix always in the red, the reverberations of a four-track on fire. 208 are emblematic of Detroit, with a sound that's like a synthesis of the Gories, with their simple song structures, and Negative Approach — who they've opened up for — with their unfiltered rage. Though Edmonds' vocals are seldom intelligible (part of the appeal), when they are his lyrics reveal existential despair, like on "RED CAT" when he howls, "I know I'll never know who I am."

Part of what makes this scene so remarkable is the musicians' ages — all of the bands began when their members were at the twilight of their teen years and the dawn of adulthood. At a transitional time in life, the steadfast commitment to remaining creative, never succumbing to the adult world's insistence that we leave behind subcultural community, is at the core of this scene's power. Additionally, the bands put out their own music on their own labels. Forging a sense of community on independently run tape labels, like Remove Records and Painters Tapes, the bands are able to get their music out physically so that they don't need to rely on getting signed or pandering to labels.

Bruiser Brigade

Meanwhile — throughout his career — Danny Brown has headed up his collective Bruiser Brigade label. The basic conceit of the Brigade is that it's a supergroup so great that it doesn't exist, but yet, it does. In their early days, they received praise from *Pitchfork*, but have since remained a largely underground phenomenon. However, in Detroit, the Brigade are championed as one of the most inspiring creative wellsprings.

Beyond their recordings, the collective are also beloved for their Bruiser Thanksgiving shows — yearly performances that feature the posse and special guests tearing it up on Turkey Day in their home city. In 2018, I attended Bruiser Thanksgiving V at the Majestic, which featured special guests JPEGMAFIA and Valee. When it came time for his set, Brown walked up to Black Sabbath's immortal banger "Iron Man," perhaps selected to reflect his childhood love of superhero action figures, or because Detroiters' associations with factories make them metaphorical iron men. Brown proceeded to deliver a career-spanning set that featured a slew of greatest hits from his albums out at the time, the most recent being *Atrocity Exhibition*. Experiencing the tracks live, the connections between Brown's rap, rave, and punk became quite clear. This was also evident in the diverse range of subcultures represented in the crowd. The message was clear: Bruiser Brigade represents the new vanguard of Detroit music culture. In 2021 — in the spirit of Detroit's legacy of rave and repurposed space — Bruiser Thanksgiving VII was held at the Russell Industrial Center.

Though Bruiser Brigade has long sat in the shadows of Brown's solo career, that's beginning to change with 2021, marking what is undeniably the group's strongest release year yet. New additions to the roster, like Fat Ray and Bruiser Wolf, have given the group an X-factor. Ray's 2021 *Santa Barbara* is a fairly conventional old-school hip-hop affair chock-full of wicked flows and wonky Dilla-esque beats. The production's sly nod to Dilla isn't coincidental either. Back when he first started in 2004, the then-nineteen-year-old Fat Ray came up under the tutelage of Dilla. With this in mind, we can see this move as Ray paying homage and respects to his late mentor.

Hot on the heels of Ray's record came Bruiser Wolf's debut release, *Dope Game Stupid*, which was the #1 album on music platform Bandcamp for weeks. Wolf — recognizing Detroit's musical legacy — knew he had to impress, since he's representing the city where one of his favorite groups — the Temptations — came from. Armed with the most idiosyncratic delivery in contemporary hip-hop, he immediately catches one's ear. Wolf's unique, suave, singerly delivery has earned him comparisons to Suga Free and E-40, but any close listen will reveal he's his own artist. Indeed, he asserts that "Nobody sounds like this, I got my own sound, I'm a instrument." Additionally, Wolf boasts an arsenal of the most gut-busting punchlines you'll ever hear:

> They was laughin', LMAO
> It was a miracle how I whipped it like Mayo.

2021 also saw the group's longtime secret weapon ZelooperZ — a renaissance man who also paints the crew's album covers, lending their catalog a cohesive aesthetic — drop the album that is the culmination of his talents, *Van Gogh's Left Ear*. A record of highly eccentric, take-no-prisoners speaker-thumping trap, ZelooperZ proves himself as one of Detroit's unsung kings. Meanwhile, giving the collective's releases a stamp of sonic cohesion is the Bruiser Brigade's in-house producers: J.U.S., SKYWLKR, and Raphy. Additionally, the crew ropes in Detroit jack-of-all-genres techno producer Black Noi$e for assistance. Closing out the stacked year from the Brigade, other hot 2021 projects from the collective include East Coaster Quentin Ahmad DaGod's *N.O.A.H.* and J.U.S.'s *GOD GOKU JAY-Z*. With so much good stuff on offer, and the Bruiser collective showing no signs of slowing down, they are another testament to how creatively coming together results in something bigger than the sum of its parts.

Putting Detroit Trap on the Map

While Bruiser Brigade — along with Quelle Chris, Black Milk, and Apollo Brown — represent Detroit's outsider, experimental hip-hop scene, we might also note that a more traditional trap scene has been rising in recent years. The Detroit trap movement could be said to originate with crews like Eastside Chedda Boyz and Doughboyz Cashout, with their leader Payroll Giovanni, but in recent years, a slew of new blood has been turning heads from industry key players. Indeed, rappers like Payroll Giovanni, Big Sean, and Tee Grizzley paved a lane for newer talents like 42 Dugg, BabyTron, Sada Baby, Dej Loaf, Kash Doll, Babyface Ray, Icewear Vezzo, and many more. Featuring a uniquely electro bass bounce and production style, Detroit trap is marked by twin lyrical themes of raunchy irreverence and struggle-ridden storytelling. For an example of the former theme, take a listen to Sada Baby's take on Tag Team's "Whoomp! (There It Is)" with the Detroit party hit "Whole Lotta Choppas," while for evidence of the latter check Tee Grizzley's anthem "First Day Out." Opening the iconic track, Grizzley rhetorically asks, "You ever been inside a federal courtroom" or "fought for your life?" Moreover, this fresh crop of talent has earned endorsements and features from out of state, in the form of Atlanta authorities on the genre, Future and Lil Baby, as well as hometown support from Eminem and Big Sean. As an example, this is the case of 42 Dugg.

Born Dion Marquise Hayes, 42's story is — in archetypically Detroit fashion — one of resilience. Arrested at fifteen years old for carjacking, Hayes would spend six life-altering years in jail. The experience would manifest in his music in the form of pleas to free friends and critiques of tough jail sentences. While spending time in solitary confinement, Hayes kept himself sane by teaching himself to rap and rhyme. When he emerged from the hole and back out on the streets of the D, he took it upon himself to start making music. While releasing Detroit bangers like "Dog Food," he was simultaneously forging connections down South with Lil Baby. By 2020, Dugg would lend his voice to two of Baby's biggest hits — "Grace" and "We Paid." As of

2022, on YouTube, the former track has 150 million clicks and the latter has garnered 330 million.

With national recognition, Dugg would also land a spot on Big Sean's posse cut "Friday Night Cypher," which also featured Tee Grizzly, Drego, Kash Doll, Cash Kidd, Payroll Giovanni, Boldy James, Sada Baby, Royce da 5'9, and Eminem. Following this, Dugg released his summer album, *Free Dem Boyz*. Featuring artwork of his incarcerated friends, *Free Dem Boyz* is a call for their release. Descending from a long lineage of Detroit music, it's music as protest and a call for freedom. With the Scorpions-sampling banger alongside Roddy Rich, "4 Da Gang," and the anthemic "Maybach" with Future, 42 Dugg had released a project that proved himself as one of Detroit's leading voices.

Flint: A Burgeoning Trap Scene

Just an hour away from Detroit lies another paradigmatic city of American neglect: Flint, Michigan. All through my high school years, I can recall turning on the television after school and seeing local news stories covering Flint's water contamination crisis. The coverage was traumatizing, seeing children my own age having their everyday life turned upside down as the poisonous water ripped through the community just north of where I lived. Of course, the government looking for a shortcut to profits was to blame for the contamination, and that, combined with the lack of response in the wake of the disaster, makes the incident one of the most notable examples of twenty-first-century environmental racism.

In recent years, Flint has come through with one of the most head-turning hip-hop scenes in the country. Flint's irreverent trap scene takes Detroit's raunchy lyricism to the next level — sometimes for better and sometimes for worse — with staples Rio Da Young OG, RMC Mike, and YN Jay.

What we ought to mention here is that, if Flint shows us anything, it is that there are many other Acid Detroit's out there. The phenomenon of destructive deindustrialization paired with neoliberal domination not only ripped through America's Rust Belt in cities like Buffalo, Cincinnati, and Toledo, but around the globe too. In Britain, there is the correlate to America's Rust Belt region known somewhat ominously and vaguely as "the North," with cities like Manchester, Salford, Leeds, and more. In Italy, there is Turin, which has eerily been dubbed "the Detroit of Italy". How many new worlds have come and gone in these places? What Psychedelic Shacks and Fun Houses might we find if we apply the same level of time and care to these similarly neglected cities? The answer is out there...

9. CODA

Well now that's done: and I'm glad it's over.
When lovely woman stoops to folly
and paces about her room again, alone,
She smoothes her hair with automatic hand,
And puts a record on the gramophone.
"This music crept by me upon the waters"
                                    T.S. Eliot, *The Waste Land*

It's a blazing hot Friday afternoon in early July, and I've
just gotten off of work. When leaving for the day, drenched
in sweat like this, I'm just grateful for the coolness of the
evening that lies ahead. I don't have particularly high
expectations for the night, but spending the evening in
Detroit with my longtime friend Jojo always contains
the promise of good music, cold drink, savory food, and
collective dancing. We don't have a plan, but our endless
options get met, thinking about some of the possibilities.
Perhaps our friends in garage punk bands are playing a gig at
UFO Factory, PJ's Lager House, or someone's house where
we'll all pile into the basement-turned-venue. Or maybe
we'll end up dancing to some local DJs spinning soulful
house, disco, or techno at Spot Lite or Tangent Gallery.
If none of that, we may be feeling creative ourselves and
head to one of our friends' studios at the Russell Industrial
Center, where we can improvise some new songs, trade
instruments throughout the night, test out lineup
combinations with whoever happens to be around.
    Arriving at my destination, I snap out of my reverie and

park my car. Midtown. Across the street is local brewery Jolly Pumpkin, Detroit-based watch company Shinola, the burned-down restaurant Traffic Jam, and Third Man Records. Jojo's just getting off of work at Third Man's pressing plant. The energy is electric down here. It's a holiday weekend and the workers are off early, having a sort of employee kickback with beer and catering. "Yes," I think to myself, "we're all off work now, and we have Monday off. The long weekend is here. We have all the time in the world, and by god, the night is ours for the taking!" A jolt of electric energy zaps my bones and I'm smiling just thinking of what awaits.

Jojo comes out of work smiling. We hug and talk about our weeks for a moment. I'm informed the plan is first to head to their apartment. Out of my car's trunk, I haul out my bicycle, which we'll be using to travel around the city this evening. After many discussions about the tyranny of cars and the way we're always tethered to these gas-guzzling machines, we've been making a conscious effort to cycle more. There are many perks to this change of transportation, and chief among them is simply that bicycling through the city is fun. Never mind the fact that we can get home from the clubs without worrying about calling a cab or relying on a designated driver, biking is enjoyable.

We reach Jojo's in Hamtramck, my favorite neighborhood in the city. Their apartment is a sort of gothic safe haven. On the walls are Twilight Zone and Joy Division posters; on the bookshelf, Mary Shelley's *Frankenstein*; above the couch, a mounted candelabra and hanging lab coat. More friends arrive and we exchange the customary greetings, but not much needs to be said. Everyone is content, decompressing and getting set for the night ahead.

First, we head to the good old Outer Limits Lounge. We've been informed that some local punk bands are playing, and we're sold at that. We step out onto the streets, pump our bikes' tires, and are off into the gleaming night. It's not far, just on the other side of Joseph Campau. We're greeted by Outer Limits' blinking neon sign, welcoming us to the Fun House. Outer Limits of consciousness. Inside is a throng of punks, mods, rockers, greasers, you name it, all jovial and joyfully exclaiming. Soundtracking the scene perfectly, tonight's Outer Limits DJs are spinning some garage rock. Sounds like maybe a record from the Cheetahs. I order a Stroh's, a beer synonymous with the city and this bar in particular. Stroh's is emblematic of Detroit excellence, and on a hot summer night the cold lager refreshes like no other. Drinks in hand, we make our way through the crowd to the back patio. Night has fallen now.

Out back in the dark is a congregation of people drinking, smoking, and waiting around for the next band to start up. We sit over by the chapel that's at the back of the patio. Someone tells us that the little chapel is actually being used the following night for a wedding. This really is a place of love and community. I'm happy, and seeing so many familiar faces around without planning anything has me smiling.

After talking with some friends, who are reminiscing about a Halloween show where they played a sloppy set of punkified Beatles tunes, we head back inside to catch the band playing.

The group is a classic Detroit affair. Their sound is raw and straight to the point, but they're also groovy. I'm picking up on influences like the Clash and Bauhaus, and some heavier stuff like Poison Idea, whom the guitarist is repping a T-shirt from. As a Detroit band, it goes without saying that the Stooges, the Gories, and Negative Approach are in their DNA too. Their energy hits the crowd right — it boils over and some leather-jacketed rockers start up a mosh, the age-old dance of punks, a controlled chaos that looks like violence, but is actually a carefully choreographed frenzy of solidarity. I'm full of life now, and jump in the pit to do some pogo dancing jumps, and we're all really howling. When the band finishes their set, I'm talking to Jojo and we know we want to dance some more. A flyer we saw earlier informed us that Marble Bar, one of the many great dance clubs in the city, is having an all-night dance party. The night is young, and we're back on the road.

Back on the cycles, we're cruising to Marble, which is about twenty minutes away. Earlier it was hot, but now it's cool, windy, and dark. As we pedal through the night, the chill of the air invigorates me. I haven't said much tonight, and Jojo asks me how I'm feeling. Sincerely, I say, "I feel alright!" We coast along.

Approaching the club, turning on to Holden, we pass the legendary Motown Museum. The iconic Hitsville, USA, itself. It's bizarre to think that we're cruising to through the same streets where Marvin, Aretha, Smokey, Diana, and all the rest would have been recording their mighty Motown hits. Sixty years later, their ghosts remain here, as two outsider kids bike up to a techno club.

From outside of Marble, we can hear the bass rattling the walls, and a second wind really kicks in. The security guard says he'll watch over our bikes, which we've linked to a fence. We thank him, and head inside. Like Outer Limits, Marble is packed to the brim, but with a whole different sort of clientele. Here we have neon ravers and unabashedly queer-presenting dancers. Like Outer Limits, there is a cross-generational community here too. Millennial couples and boomers in fedoras doing the robot are alongside early twenty-somethings rolling — dosed on Molly — for the first time. The music is absolutely kicking. Though we usually get old-school techno inspired by Detroit royalty at Marble, tonight the music sounds more inspired by Larry Levan's disco sets at the Paradise Garage. Jojo and I nestle up right next to the subwoofer speaker upfront and break into dance. The music is taking me high tonight, and I really lock into the groove, jerkily convulsing my body, hanging on every drop. Taking cues from Detroit's Moodymann, the DJ is spinning an eclectic mix over the quintessential house beat, "Contort Yourself" by James White & the Blacks, which segues into a mixed version of the new Drake record "Falling Back," which is followed by Jojo's favorite: "Gypsy Woman" by Crystal Waters. The set culminates with an excellent surprise when the most famous piano chord in music history hits, "Bennie and the Jets" by Elton John bursts through the speakers over the thumping house beat. Everybody on the floor is dialed in with hands up, and we're hollering:

> Hey kids shake it loose together
> The Spotlights hitting something that's been known to change the weather
> We'll kill the fatted calf tonight so stick around
> You're gonna hear electric music, solid walls of sound

With that, we're experiencing a collective ecstasy. The room is radiant.

I've turned twenty-three just a week ago, and I know my youth is dwindling. It'll all be over in a flash, but tonight the time is free and unpressured. Clouds of smoke are puffing up as crews pass joints around. The kids on molly are possessed, dancing with clenched jaws and dilated eye. A psychedelic shack, that's where we're at. Everyone's here. No hierarchies or judging, just dancing. Expressive arts therapy. Now, Jojo and I acknowledge each other in the dance.

"I'm lifted!"

"Yes, my spirits are up!"

"Up up up! We're high up!"

Once again, but only to myself, I repeat, "I feel alright." *I feel alright*. Great friends, a sacred bond here.

After the dance, outside now, we sit on the stoop of a dilapidated, emptied-out house next door. Typical in Detroit. In Jojo's bag is a copy of Simon Reynolds' book *Generation Ecstasy*, a raver's bible that traces the many pilgrimages, meccas, and mutations our city's music has undertaken. Evangelists of the E-Generation, we know that it all started here on this street, with Motown's music composed to the clanks of the assembly line. We live to tell the tale.

It's Fourth of July weekend, and we patriots of Detroit hop back on the bikes. As we coast back into Hamtramck, the sound of birds chirping are beginning to sound. Momentarily, the straight world will begin waking up to starts its Saturday morning, and I realize that we've really been out all night without thinking twice about it. In fact, we're not even tired. On the contrary, *we're wired*. Jojo invites me into their second-floor apartment and we pop out onto their balcony, which overlooks the city. The birds are still chirping, singing us a lullaby as the sun begins to rise. We don't speak, just stare out over the horizon, coming down.

Each dawn we die, but we always rise from the ashes of this once-scorched earth.

THE MUSIC OF ACID DETROIT

1. FORDIST MOTOWN

"Shop Around" — The Miracles (1960)
"My Guy" — Mary Wells (1964)
Where Did Our Love Go — The Supremes (1964)
"Dancing in the Street" — Martha & the Vandellas (1964)
"My Girl" — The Temptations (1964)
"The Tracks of My Tears" — The Miracles (1965)
"Nowhere to Run" — Martha & the Vandellas (1965)
Up-Tight Everything's Alright — Stevie Wonder (1966)
"I Second That Emotion" — The Miracles (1967)

2. REVOLUTIONARY PROTOPUNKERS

"Never Thought You'd Leave Me"/"What A Way to Die" — The Pleasure Seekers (1965)
"96 Tears" — ? & The Mysterians (1966)
Kick Out the Jams — MC5 (1969)
The Stooges — The Stooges (1969)
Fun House — The Stooges (1970)
Back in the U.S.A. — MC5 (1970)
Cold Fact — Rodriguez (1970)
Coming From Reality — Rodriguez (1971)
Suzi Quatro — Suzi Quatro (1973)
...For the Whole World to See — Death (1975)
The Idiot — Iggy Pop (1977)
Lust for Life — Iggy Pop (1977)

"Bored / You're Gonna Die" — Destroy All Monsters (1978)
"City Slang" — Sonic's Rendezvous Band (1978)

3. PSYCHEDELIC SOUL

"Reflections" — The Supremes (1967)
"I Wanna Testify" — The Parliaments (1967)
"I Heard it Through the Grapevine" — Marvin Gaye (1968)
"Love Child" — The Supremes (1968)
Cloud Nine — The Temptations (1969)
Hair and Thangs — The Dennis Coffey Trio (1969)
Puzzle People — The Temptations (1969)
"War" — Edwin Starr (1970)
Psychedelic Shack — The Temptations (1970)
New Ways But Love Stays — The Supremes (1970)
Free Your Mind... And Your Ass Will Follow — Funkadelic (1970)
Maggot Brain — Funkadelic (1971)
The Undisputed Truth — Undisputed Truth (1971)
Evolution — Dennis Coffey & the Detroit Guitar Band (1971)
Talking Book — Stevie Wonder (1972)
Face to Face With the Truth — Undisputed Truth (1972)
What's Going On — Marvin Gaye (1971)
Let's Get it On — Marvin Gaye (1973)
Innervisions — Stevie Wonder (1973)
Fulfillingness' First Finale — Stevie Wonder (1974)
I Want You — Marvin Gaye (1975)
Stepping Into Tomorrow — Donald Byrd (1975)
Places & Spaces — Donald Byrd (1975)
Songs in the Key of Life — Stevie Wonder (1976)

4. ELECTRIC ENTOURAGE

"Autobahn" — Kraftwerk (1975)
Trans-Europe Express — Kraftwerk (1977)
The Man Machine — Kraftwerk (1978)
Replicas — Gary Numan (1978)
The Pleasure Principle — Gary Numan (1979)
"Sharevari" — A Number of Names (1981)
"Alleys of Your Mind" — Cybotron (1981)
Enter — Cybotron (1983)
"No UFOs / Future" — Model 500 (1985)
"Nude Photo / The Dance" — Rhythim Is Rhythim
"Strings of Life" — Rhythim Is Rhythim (1987)
"Good Life" — Inner City (1988)
Techno: The New Dance Sound of Detroit — Various
Artists (1988)
The Final Frontier — Underground Resistance (1991)
Message to the Majors — Underground Resistance (1992)
Drexciya 4: The Unknown Aquazone — Drexciya (1994)
More Songs About Food and Revolutionary Art — Carl
Craig (1997)
Interstellar Fugitives — UR (1998)
Neptune's Lair — Drexciya (1999)
"Inspiration / Transition" — Underground
Resistance (2002)
Harnessed the Storm — Drexciya (2002)

5. HARDCORE TIMES

Easy Action — Alice Cooper (1970)
Love it to Death — Alice Cooper (1971)
Killer — Alice Cooper (1972)
Billion Dollar Babies — Alice Cooper (1973)
"Detroit Rock City" — Kiss (1976)

"Sex Drive" — Necros (1981)
"I.Q. 32" — Necros (1981)
L-Seven — L-Seven (1982)
Tied Down — Negative Approach (1983)
Conquest for Death — Necros (1983)
Merry-Go-Round — Laughing Hyenas (1987)
You Can't Pray A Lie — Laughing Hyenas (1989)
Life of Crime — Laughing Hyenas (1990)
Crawl — Laughing Hyenas (1992)
Hard Times — Laughing Hyenas (1995)
Easy Action — Easy Action (2001)
Friends of Rock & Roll — Easy Action (2005)
Toothpaste & Pills — Static (2021)

6. TIME OUT OF JOINT

Houserockin' — The Gories (1989)
I Know You Fine, But How You Doin' — The Gories (1990)
Outta Here — The Gories (1992)
Fan-tas-tic — Slum Village (1997)
Deal Me In — Bantam Rooster (1997)
Mink, Rat or Rabbit — The Detroit Cobras (1998)
The White Stripes — The White Stripes (1999)
De Stijl — The White Stripes (2000)
Fan-tas-tic Vol. 2 — Slum Village (2000)
Ultraglide in Black — The Dirtbombs (2001)
Life, Love and Leaving — The Detroit Cobras (2001)
White Blood Cells — The White Stripes (2001)
Welcome 2 Detroit — J Dilla (2001)
Dangerous Magical Noise — The Dirtbombs (2003)
Elephant — The White Stripes (2003)
Baby — The Detroit Cobras (2004)
Get Behind Me, Satan — The White Stripes (2005)
Donuts — J Dilla (2006)
Party Store — The Dirtbombs (2011)

The Shaw Tapes: Live in Detroit 5/27/88 — The Gories (2013)
Live at Outer Limits — The Stools (2020)

7. ACID RAP

Boomin' Words from Hell — Esham (1989)
Judgement Day — Esham (1992)
KKKill the Fetus — Esham (1993)
The Great Milenko — Insane Clown Posse (1997)
The Slim Shady LP — Eminem (1999)
Detroit State of Mind — Danny Brown (2007)
The Hybrid — Danny Brown (2010)
XXX — Danny Brown (2012)
Old — Danny Brown (2013)
Atrocity Exhibition — Danny Brown (2016)
Time Crisis — Black Noi$e (2017)
Illusions — Black Noi$e (2018)
uknowhatimsayin? — Danny Brown (2019)

8. POST-CAPITALIST DETROIT

Together Now — Toeheads (2019)
Santa Barbara — Fat Ray (2021)
Dope Game Stupid — Bruiser Wolf (2021)
Van Gogh's Left Ear — ZelooperZ (2021)
TV62 — Bruiser Brigade (2021)
Free Dem Boyz — 42 Dugg (2021)
Face — Babyface Ray (2022)
NEARBY — 208 (2022)

THE FILMS OF ACID DETROIT

Finally Got The News... — Stewart Bird, Peter Gessner, René Lichtman, John Louis Jr. (1970)

Two Lane Blacktop — Monte Hellman (1971)
Blue Collar — Paul Schrader (1978)
RoboCop — Paul Verhoeven (1987)
Zebrahead — Anthony Dravis (1992)
8 Mile — Curtis Hanson (2002)
The Cycles of The Mental Machine — Jacqueline Caux (2006)
We Are Not Ghosts — Mark Dworkin, Melissa Young (2011)
Only Lovers Left Alive — Jim Jarmusch (2013)
Lost River — Ryan Gosling (2014)

Repeater Books

is dedicated to the creation of a new reality. The landscape of twenty-first-century arts and letters is faded and inert, riven by fashionable cynicism, egotistical self-reference and a nostalgia for the recent past. Repeater intends to add its voice to those movements that wish to enter history and assert control over its currents, gathering together scattered and isolated voices with those who have already called for an escape from Capitalist Realism. Our desire is to publish in every sphere and genre, combining vigorous dissent and a pragmatic willingness to succeed where messianic abstraction and quiescent co-option have stalled: abstention is not an option: we are alive and we don't agree